IRAQ: THE BORROWED KETTLE

WO ES WAR

A series from Verso edited by Slavoj Žižek

Wo es war, soll ich werden — Where it was, I shall come into being — is Freud's version of the Enlightenment goal of knowledge that is in itself an act of liberation. Is it still possible to pursue this goal today, in the conditions of late capitalism? If 'it' today is the twin rule of pragmatic-relativist New Sophists and New Age obscurantists, what 'shall come into being' in its place? The premiss of the series is that the explosive combination of Lacanian psychoanalysis and Marxist tradition detonates a dynamic freedom that enables us to question the very presuppositions of the circuit of Capital.

In the same series:

IRAQ:
THE BORROWED KETTLE

SLAVOJ ŽIŽEK

VERSO

London · New York

First published by Verso 2004

1 3 5 7 9 10 8 6 4 2

Verso
UK: 6 Meard Street, London W1F 0EG
USA: 180 Varick Street, New York, NY 10014–4606
www.versobooks.com

Verso is the imprint of New Left Books

ISBN 1–84467–001–5

British Library Cataloguing in Publication Data
Žižek, Slavoj
    Iraq : the borrowed kettle
    1.War on Terrorism, 2001– 2.Iraq War, 2003 – Causes
    3. Political science – Philosophy
    I.Title
    909.8'3
    ISBN 1844670015

Library of Congress Cataloging-in-Publication Data
    Žižek, Slavoj
        Iraq : the borrowed kettle / Slavoj Žižek.
        p. cm. – (Wo es war)
    includes bibliographical references
    ISBN 1–84467–001–5 (hardcover : alk. paper)
    1. Iraq War, 2003. I. Title. II. Series.
    DS79.76.Z595 2004
    956.7044'3–dc22   2004004630

Typeset in Perpetua by YHT Ltd, London
Printed and bound in the USA by R. R. Donnelley & Sons

For Alenka Zupančič and Mladen Dolar,
the two other members of my party *troika*.

CONTENTS

Introduction: They Control Iraq, But Do They Control Themselves?

> Of course the people don't want war. . . . . But after all, it is the leaders of the country who determine the policy, and it's always a simple matter to drag the people along. . . . All you have to do is tell them they are being attacked, and denounce the pacifists for lack of patriotism and exposing the country to danger. It works the same in any country.
> (Hermann Goering, speaking at the Nuremberg trials in 1946)

The title of this book does not refer to the ancient kettles which disappeared from the museums and archaeological sites in the days after the collapse of Saddam Hussein's regime (in all probability, to reappear after the appropriate time first on the black, then on the legitimate, art market): these kettles were mostly stolen, not borrowed, and the worry about the looting of museums and archaeological sites in Iraq again displayed the hypocrisy and pretence of the liberal attitude of 'respect for other cultures'. The title refers to another kettle – the one in the joke evoked by Freud to illustrate the strange logic of dreams: (1) I never borrowed a kettle from you; (2) I returned it to you unbroken; (3) the kettle was already broken when I got it from you. Such an enumeration of inconsistent arguments, of course, confirms *per negationem* what it endeavours to deny – that I returned a broken kettle to you.

Did not the same inconsistency characterize the justification of the war on Iraq in early 2003? (1) Saddam Hussein possesses weapons of mass destruction which pose a 'clear and present

danger' not only to his neighbours and Israel, but to all democratic Western states. (2) So what were we to do when, in
September 2003, David Kay, the CIA official in charge of the
search for weapons of mass destruction (WMDs) in Iraq, had to
concede that no such weapons had been found so far (after more
than a thousand US specialists had spent months looking for
them)? We move on to the next level: even if Saddam does not
have any WMDs, he was involved with al-Qaeda in the 9/11
attack, so he should be punished as part of the justified revenge
for 9/11 and in order to prevent such attacks in the future. (3)
However, again, in September 2003, even President George Bush
had to concede: 'We have no evidence that Saddam Hussein was
involved with the September 11 attacks.' So what do we do after
this painful concession, given the fact that a recent opinion poll
found that nearly 70 per cent of Americans believed the Iraqi
leader was personally involved in those attacks? We move on to
the next level: even if there is no proof of the link with al-Qaeda,
Saddam's regime is a ruthless dictatorial regime, a threat to its
neighbours and a catastrophe to its own people, and this fact alone
provides reason enough to topple it. . . .[1] The problem, again,
was that there were *too many* reasons for the war.

What conferred a semblance of consistency on this multitude of
reasons was, of course, ideology. The images of Saddam endlessly
repeated on our screens before the war (Saddam firing a rifle into
the air) made him into some kind of Iraqi Charlton Heston – the
president not only of Iraq, but also of the Iraqi Rifle Association.
. . . The true interest of these images, however, is that they
remind us how the ideological struggle is fought out not only at
the level of arguments but also at the level of images: which image

will hegemonize a field, and function as the paradigmatic embodiment of an idea, a regime, a problem. Recall (the now half-
forgotten) Jessica Lynch, 'the face of the war': in an ideological
gesture *par excellence*, she was elevated into the paradigm of the
US soldier. Her story is to be read at three levels, which again
correspond to the Lacanian triad Imaginary–Symbolic–Real (ISR).
First there was the imaginary spectacle: the ordinary all-American
girl-next-door, tender and fragile, the very opposite of the brutish
soldier of our imagination. . . . Then, of course, there was, the
underlying ideological background, the symbolic level of media
manipulation. And, last but not least, we should not forget the
very 'vulgar' economic aspect: Jessica enlisted in the US Army in
order to be able to pursue her studies afterwards, that is, to *escape*
the small-town lower-class life of a rural community in crisis, so
that when she 'triumphantly' returned home, this looked more
like being brought back to a prison from which she had tried to
break out – no wonder she looked uneasy, and the spectacle of
her homecoming did not really catch on.[2]

In contrast to the Gulf War of 1991, epitomized by the camera
shot of a computer-guided projectile hitting its target, thereby
depicting war as an abstract computer game (there were no
battlefield reports during that war; the blackout was complete),
the Iraqi war of 2003 was well characterized by the 'embedded
reporters' – reporters staying with the troops, providing live
coverage of their day-to-day life and the battles themselves, thus
contributing the 'human touch' and generating an instant identification of the spectator's perspective with that of the soldier.
With regard to this shift, it is crucial to note how *both* approaches
are 'abstract' in the strict Hegelian–Marxian sense – if anything,

there is *more* truth about the actual nature of the war in the abstract-technological video-game approach. The 'concrete' depiction of the experience of combatants is abstract in the sense that it obfuscates the concrete totality which provides the true global meaning of the war. What, then, would have been the correct approach? Apropos of this war reporting, I am tempted to repeat the old Adornian critical comment: the truth is the very split between the two modes, the abstract-digital level and the 'human-touch' level of individual experience – in other words, the truth is that this split is irreducible, that there is no common denominator between the two.[3]

What, then, was the real reason for going to war? Strangely, there were, in effect, three: (1) a sincere ideological belief that the USA was bringing democracy and prosperity to another nation; (2) the urge brutally to assert and demonstrate uncon-ditional US hegemony; (3) control of Iraq's oil reserves. Each of the three levels has a relative autonomy of its own, and should not be dismissed as a mere deceptive semblance. Recall the basic American reaction (at least) since the Vietnam War: we just try to do good, to help others, to bring peace and prosperity, and look what we get in return. . . . The fundamental insight of movies like John Ford's *Searchers* and Michael Scorsese's *Taxi Driver* is today, with the global American ideological offensive, more relevant than ever – we witness the resurgence of the figure of the 'quiet American', a naive benevolent agent who sincerely wants to bring democracy and Western freedom to the Vietnamese; it is just that his intentions totally misfire, or, as Graham Greene put it: 'I never knew a man who had better motives for all the trouble he caused.'

As for the second reason, in their recent *The War Over Iraq*, William Kristol and Lawrence F. Kaplan wrote:

> The mission begins in Baghdad, but it does not end there. . . . We stand at the cusp of a new historical era. . . . This is a decisive moment. . . . It is so clearly about more than Iraq. It is about more even than the future of the Middle East and the war on terror. It is about what sort of role the United States intends to play in the twenty-first century.

I can only agree with this: it truly is the future of the international community that is at stake now − the new rules that will regulate it; the character of the New World Order.

As far as oil is concerned, as reported in the media in June 2003, Paul Wolfowitz not only dismissed the WMD issue as a 'bureaucratic' excuse for war, but openly admitted that oil was the true motive: 'Let's look at it simply. The most important difference between North Korea and Iraq is that economically, we just had no choice in Iraq. The country swims on a sea of oil.'[4] And it seems obvious that the key factor was the middle one: using Iraq as a pretext or an exemplary case to stake out the co-ordinates of the New World Order, to assert the USA's right to pre-emptive strikes, and thus to elevate its status into that of the only global policeman. The message was addressed not to the Iraqi people, but primarily to all of us, the witnesses to the war − we were its true ideological and political targets.

A new vision of the New World order is thus emerging as the *de facto* guiding light of recent US politics: after September 11, the USA basically wrote off the rest of the world as a reliable partner; the ultimate goal is therefore no longer the Fukuyama utopia of expanding universal liberal democracy, but the transformation of the USA into 'Fortress America', a lone superpower isolated from the rest of the world, protecting its vital economic interests and securing its safety through its new military power, which includes not only forces for rapid deployment anywhere around the globe, but also the development of space weapons by means of which the USA will control the surface of the globe from above. The existence of this strategy throws a new light on to the recent conflicts between the USA and Europe: it is not Europe which is 'betraying' the USA; the USA itself no longer needs or has to rely on its exclusive partnership with Europe. While this vision, of course, is an ideological fiction (today, the idea that any country can be a secluded 'fortress' is quite simply unworkable), it is none the less a fiction with immense material power, a fiction materialized in gigantic state apparatuses, and economic and military activity.

Iraq: The Borrowed Kettle focuses on the background that such inconsistent argumentation conceals and, simultaneously, cannot but point towards – that is to say, what it reveals in the very gesture of concealment. The three 'true' reasons for the attack on Iraq (ideological belief in Western democracy – Bush's 'democracy is God's gift to humanity'; the assertion of US hegemony in the New World Order; economic interests – oil) should be treated like a 'parallax': it is not that one is the 'truth' of the others; the 'truth' is, rather, the very shift of perspective between them. They relate to each other like the ISR triad mentioned above: the Imaginary of democratic ideology, the Symbolic of political hegemony, the Real of the economy, and, as Lacan would have put it in his late works, they are knotted together. In its two appendices, this book thus follows the path of gradual 'abstraction' from direct political analysis (or, rather, in Hegelese, the path towards concrete totality): first, it questions the reference to democracy and its defence, which plays the central role in the justification for the war; then it goes into a more fundamental problem of the structure of domination that characterizes the contemporary social order.

The hidden literary model for this book is what I consider E.L. Doctorow's masterpiece, the supreme exercise in literary postmodernism, far superior to his bestselling *Ragtime*, or *Billy Bathgate*; his *Lives of the Poets: Six Stories and a Novella* – six totally heterogeneous short stories (a son is set the task of concealing his father's death; a drowned child is callously handled by rescuers; a lonely schoolteacher is shot by a hunter; a boy witnesses his mother's act of infidelity; a car explosion kills a foreign schoolgirl) accompanied by a novella which conveys the confused impressions of the day-to-day life of a writer in contemporary New York who, as we soon guess, is the author of the six stories. The charm of the book is that we can reconstruct the process of the artistic working-through of the raw material of this day-to-day life. In the same way, the main chapter of *Iraq: The Borrowed Kettle* is a *bric-à-brac* of the author's immediate impressions and reactions to the unfolding story of the US attack on Iraq, followed by two appendices which provide more consistent theoretical analyses distilled from the immediate reactions to the Iraqi war: democracy and its discontents, the contemporary logic of domination (the shift from the Master's discourse to the University discourse).

So, in the style of Magritte's *Ceci n'est pas une pipe*, I should emphasize that *Iraq: The Borrowed Kettle* is not a book about Iraq – but the Iraqi crisis and war were not really about Iraq either. What one should resist apropos of Iraq is thus the *temptation of false concreteness*: 'A terrible dictator was overthrown – what's so bad about that!' Or – a more elaborate version – 'After the Communist attempts to do good, which ended catastrophically, is it not preferable to have an act that may have bad motives (oil, imperialist hegemony), but good results?' Michael Ignatieff wrote recently: 'For me the key issue is what would be the best result for the Iraqi people – what is most likely to improve the human rights of 26 million Iraqis? What always drove me crazy about the opposition [to the war] was that it was never about Iraq. It was a referendum on American power.'[5] Paul Berman made the same point: 'What we need to do is try and persuade people that this is not a war about Bush but about totalitarianism in the Middle East.'[6] One should counter such statements with a naive question: do Ignatieff and Berman seriously believe that the US attack on Iraq was motivated by the desire 'to improve the human rights of 26 million Iraqis'? Even if the improvement of life for the Iraqis may be a welcome 'collateral' effect of the overthrow of Saddam's regime, can any serious analysis be allowed to forget the global context of the attack on Iraq, the new rules of international life that were exemplified and imposed by this attack? *This* – not sympathy for Saddam, nor abstract pacifism – was what moved millions in Western Europe to demonstrate against the war.

One of the pop heroes of the USA–Iraq war was undoubtedly Muhammed Saeed al-Sahaf, the unfortunate Iraqi Information Minister who, in his daily press conferences, heroically denied even the most evident facts, and stuck to the Iraqi line – when the US tanks were only a few hundred yards from his office, he continued to claim that the US TV shots of tanks on the Baghdad streets were just Hollywood special effects. In his very functioning as an excessive caricature, he thereby revealed the hidden truth of 'normal' reporting: there was no refined spin to his comments, just a plain denial. There was something refreshing and liberating about his interventions, which displayed a striving emancipated from the grip of facts, and thus of the need to spin away their unpleasant aspects; his stance was one of 'Whom do you believe, your eyes or my words?' Furthermore, sometimes he even hit on a strange truth. For example, confronted with claims that the Americans were in control of parts of Baghdad, he snapped back: 'They aren't in control of anything – they don't even control themselves!'

Why not? In March 2003, Donald Rumsfeld engaged in a little bit of amateur philosophizing about the relationship between the known and the unknown:

> There are known knowns. These are things we know that we know. There are known unknowns. That is to say, there are things that we know we don't know. But there are also unknown unknowns. There are things we don't know we don't know.

What he forgot to add was the crucial fourth term: the 'unknown knowns', the things we do not know that we know – which is precisely the Freudian unconscious, the 'knowledge which does not know itself', as Lacan used to say. If Rumsfeld thinks that the main dangers in the confrontation with Iraq are the 'unknown unknowns', the threats from Saddam whose existence we do not even suspect, we should reply that the main dangers are, on the contrary, the 'unknown knowns', the disavowed beliefs and suppositions we are not even aware of adhering to ourselves. These disavowed beliefs and suppositions – which America (the US political elite) does not control, since it is unaware of their very existence – are the ultimate topic of this book.

Non Penis a Pendendo

The Iraqi MacGuffin

We all know what the Hitchcockian 'MacGuffin' is: the empty pretext which just serves to set the story in motion, but has no value in itself; in order to illustrate it, Hitchcock often quoted the following story:

> Two gentlemen meet on a train, and one is struck by the extraordinary package being carried by the other. He asks his companion, 'What is in that unusual package you are carrying there?' The other man replies, 'That is a MacGuffin.' 'What is a MacGuffin?' asks the first man. The second says, 'A MacGuffin is a device used for killing leopards in the Scottish highlands.' Naturally the first man says, 'But there are no leopards in the Scottish highlands.' 'Well,' says the second, 'then that's not a MacGuffin, is it?'

Do not the 'Iraqi weapons of mass destruction' fit the profile of the MacGuffin perfectly? (Incidentally, one of the most famous Hitchcockian MacGuffins *is* a potential weapon of mass destruction – the bottles with 'radioactive diamonds' in *Notorious*!) Are they not also an elusive entity, never empirically specified? When, a couple of years ago, the UN inspectors were searching for them in Iraq, they were expected to be hidden in the most disparate and improbable places, from the desert (a rather logical location) to the (slightly irrational) cellars of the presidential palaces (so that, when the palace was bombed, they would poison Saddam and his entire entourage?), allegedly present in large quantities, yet, as if by magic, manually moved around all the time by teams of workers. The more these weapons were destroyed, the more omnipresent and omnipotent their menace seemed, as if the destruction of the greater part of them supernaturally augmented the destructive power of the remainder. As such, by definition, they can never be found, and are therefore all the more dangerous. . . . Now that none have been found, we have reached the last line of the MacGuffin story: ' "Well," said President Bush in September 2003, "then that's not a MacGuffin, is it?" '

In autumn 2003, when, after hundreds of investigators had searched high and low for WMDs, yet not a single one had been located, the public were posing the elementary question: 'If there are no WMDs, why did we attack Iraq? Did you lie to us?' No wonder the search for WMDs is gradually being elevated into a modern version of the search for the Holy Grail – David Kay, the CIA analyst who, in September 2003, wrote the report admitting that no weapons were to be found, qualified this concession by adding that it was too early to reach definitive conclusions, and much work remained to be done: 'I think they'll be digging up the relics of Saddam Hussein's empire for the next hundred years.' Tony Blair, a passionate Christian, has expressed his conviction that WMDs will be found in almost directly religious terms of *credo qua absurdum*: despite the lack of evidence, he personally is deeply convinced that they will be found. . . . The only appropriate answer to this conundrum is not the boring liberal plea for innocence until guilt is proved but, rather, the point made succinctly by 'Rachel from Scotland' on the BBC website in September 2003: 'We know he had weapons; we sold him some of them.' This is the direction a serious investigation should have taken.

The problem with the basic refrain ('Iraq is a big country, Saddam had lots of time to hide the WMDs, so give us more time and we will definitely find them!') is that its structure is the same as that of a judge who first punishes the accused and then, forced to admit that he has no proof that the crime has in fact been committed, says: 'Give me more time, and I promise you I will find material proof that will justify my punishment!' So – first you punish, then you look for proof of the crime. Not to mention the fact that this, precisely, was what the UN weapons inspectors were asking for before the war – more time – but were scathingly dismissed by the USA. On the basis of all these facts, I am tempted to entertain the hypothesis that the Americans were not simply unsure whether Saddam had WMDs or not, but that they positively knew he did *not* have them – which is why they risked the ground offensive on Iraq. For, had the USA taken seriously its own claims that Iraq possessed WMDs which could be unleashed immediately, it probably would not have launched a ground assault, fearing too many casualties on its own side, but would have stuck to an air-bombardment campaign.

Here, then, we have the first practical demonstration of what the Bush doctrine of preventive strikes means, a doctrine now publicly declared as the official American 'philosophy' of international politics (in the thirty-one-page paper entitled 'The National Security Strategy' issued by the White House on 20 September 2002). Its main points are: American military might should remain 'beyond challenge' in the foreseeable future; since the main enemy today is an 'irrational' fundamentalist who, unlike the Communists, lacks even an elementary sense of survival and respect for his own people, America has the right to preemptive strikes (that is, to attack countries which do not already pose a clear threat to the USA, but *might* pose such a threat in the *foreseeable* future); while the USA should seek to build *ad hoc* international coalitions for such attacks, it should reserve the right to act independently if it does not receive sufficient international support. So, while the USA presents its domination of other sovereign states as grounded in a benevolent paternalism which takes into account the interests of other nations and their peoples, it reserves for itself the ultimate right to *define* its allies' 'true' interests. The logic is thus clearly formulated: even the pretence of neutral international law is abandoned, since, when the USA perceives a potential threat, it formally asks its allies for support, but the allies' agreement is actually optional. The underlying message is always 'We will do it with or without you' (in short, you are free to agree with us, but not free to disagree). The old paradox of the forced choice is reproduced here: the freedom to make a choice on condition that one makes the right choice.

The 'Bush doctrine' relies on the violent assertion of the paranoid logic of total control over *future* threats, justifying preemptive strikes against these supposed threats. The ineptitude of such an approach in the contemporary world, in which knowledge circulates freely, is patent. The loop between the present and the future is closed: the prospect of a breathtaking terrorist act is evoked in order to justify incessant pre-emptive strikes now. This closed loop was perfectly formulated in a TV debate in February 2002, when the actor and ex-Congressman Fred Thompson said, in defence of President Bush's Iraq politics: 'When anti-war protesters say, "But what did Iraq actually *do* to the USA? It did not attack us!", one should answer it with the question, "And what did the terrorists who destroyed the Twin Towers actually *do* to the USA before September 11? They also did nothing!" ' The problem with this logic is that it presupposes that we can treat the future as something that, in a way, has already taken place.

The ultimate paradox is that the very strategy of pre-emptive strikes will contribute to the proliferation of nuclear weapons. When the USA attacked Iraq and not North Korea, the underlying logic was clear: once a 'rogue' state has breached the critical limit and acquired substantial nuclear weapons, one cannot simply attack it because one risks a nuclear backlash killing millions on 'our' side. This, precisely, was the lesson North Korea drew from the attack on Iraq: the regime sees nuclear weapons as the only guarantee of its survival; in its view, Iraq's mistake was to accept the collaboration with the UN and the presence of international inspectors in the first place.

What, then, is the greatest danger of the American occupation of Iraq? Prior to the US attack on Iraq, everyone feared some kind of catastrophic outcome: an ecological catastrophe of gigantic proportions, high US casualties, another massive terrorist attack against the West. ... Thus we all silently accepted the US standpoint – and now, after the rapid end to the war (in a kind of repetition of the 1991 Gulf War) and the disintegration of Saddam's regime, there is a universal sigh of relief, even among many critics of US policy. I would therefore like to consider the hypothesis that, before the outbreak of the war, the USA was deliberately fomenting this fear of an impending catastrophe, counting on the universal relief when the catastrophe actually *failed* to occur. This, however, is arguably the greatest true danger. That is to say: one should have the courage to proclaim the opposite – perhaps an adverse military turn for the USA would have been the best thing that could have happened, a sobering piece of bad news which would have compelled all the participants to rethink their position.

In the days and weeks after the 'triumphant' conclusion of the war, the peace movement all but disappeared, and the Western European states which had opposed the war ducked out in shame and started to make conciliatory gestures towards the USA – Gerhardt Schröder even apologized publicly for his anti-American statements. This uneasiness of the opponents of the war is a sad sign of their deep disorientation: it is *now* that they should be really concerned. To accept that 'none the less things turned out OK', that Saddam's regime collapsed without a large number of dead and without the feared major catastrophes (the burning of oil wells, the use of weapons of mass destruction) is to succumb to the most dangerous illusion – it is here that they are paying the price for opposing the war for the wrong reasons. The line of argument which tried to demonstrate how the US occupation would hurt the Iraqis was simply wrong: if anything, ordinary Iraqis will probably ultimately *profit* from the defeat of Saddam's regime in terms of their standard of living, and religious and other freedoms. The true victims of the war are not the Iraqis, they are elsewhere!

Are we aware that, at least until now, all the predictions evoked as the justification for war have proved false? No weapons of mass destruction were used, or even discovered; there were no fanatical Arab suicide bombers (until very recently); almost no oil wells were ignited; there were no determined Republican Guard divisions defending Baghdad to the end and risking the destruction of the city – in short, Iraq proved to be a paper tiger which basically just collapsed under US pressure.[1] Is this very military 'triumph' not the ultimate proof of the fact that the opposition to the war was *justified* – that Iraq was *not* a threat to the USA? Saddam's regime was an abominable authoritarian state, guilty of many crimes, especially towards its own people. We should, however, note the key fact that when the US representatives were enumerating Saddam's evil deeds, they systematically omitted what was undoubtedly his greatest crime (in terms of human suffering and of violations of international law): the aggression against Iran. Why? Because the USA and the majority of foreign states were actively helping Iraq in this aggression. . . .

If we accept as the true aim of the attack on Iraq the struggle against Muslim fundamentalism, then we are forced to conclude that the attack was not only a failure, but it even strengthened the very cause it tried to combat. Saddam Hussein's regime in Iraq was ultimately secular and nationalist in character, out of touch with fundamentalist Muslim populism – it is obvious that Saddam only superficially flirted with pan-Arab Muslim sentiment. As his past clearly demonstrates, he was a pragmatic ruler striving for power, shifting from one alliance to another as and when it suited his purposes: first against Iran, to grab its oil fields; then against Kuwait, for the same reason, bringing upon himself a pan-Arab coalition allied to the USA. What Saddam was definitely not was a fundamentalist obsessed with the 'Great Satan', ready to blow the world apart just to strike at him. The ultimate proof of this secular nature of the Ba'ath regime is the ironic fact that – in the Iraqi elections of October 2002, in which Saddam Hussein got a 100 per cent endorsement, thereby outshining the best Stalinist results of 99.95 per cent – the campaign song played again and again on all the state media was none other than Whitney Houston's 'I Will Always Love You'.

We can surmise that the Americans were well aware that the era of Saddam and his non-fundamentalist regime was coming to an end, and that the attack on Iraq was probably conceived as a much more radical pre-emptive strike – not against Saddam, but against the main contender as Saddam's political successor: a truly fundamentalist Islamic regime. Yet, if this is so, the vicious cycle of American intervention can only get more complex. The danger, following the logic of a self-fulfilling prophecy, is that this very American intervention will contribute to the emergence of what America fears most: a large, united, anti-American Muslim front. This is the first case of a direct American occupation of a large and key Arab country – how could it not generate universal hatred in reaction? One can already imagine thousands of young people dreaming of becoming suicide bombers, and how that will force the US government to impose a state of emergency, permanently on high alert.

What might indeed emerge as the result of the US occupation is precisely a truly fundamentalist Muslim anti-American movement, directly linked to such movements in other Arab countries or countries with a Muslim presence – in other words, a Muslim 'International'. And the first signs are already discernible: from the daily Shi'ite demonstrations against the US presence in Iraq to the daily attacks on US soldiers.[2] It is as if, in a contemporary display of the 'cunning of reason', some invisible hand of destiny repeatedly arranges it so that the short-term success of the US intervention strengthens the very cause against which the USA intervened.

At this point, however, I cannot resist a slightly paranoid speculation: what if the people around Bush know all this, what if this 'collateral damage' is the true aim of the entire operation? What if the *true* target of the 'war on terror' is not only a global geopolitical rearrangement in the Middle East and beyond, but also American society itself (namely, the repression of whatever remains of its emancipatory potential)? We should therefore be very careful not to fight false battles: the debates about how evil Saddam was, even about the cost of the war, and so forth, are red herrings. The focus should be on what actually transpires in our societies, on what kind of society is emerging *here and now* as the result of the 'war on terror'. The ultimate result of the war will be a change in *our* political order.

The Nation-State Empire

At this point, one should ask a naive question: the USA as global policeman — why not? The post-Cold War situation did, in effect, call for some global power to fill the void. The problem lies elsewhere: recall the widespread perception of the USA as a new Roman Empire. *The problem with today's USA is not that it is a new global Empire, but that it is* not: *in other words, that, while pretending to be, it continues to act as a nation-state, ruthlessly pursuing its own interests.* It is as if the guiding principle of recent US politics is a weird reversal of the well-known ecologists' motto: *act globally, think locally*. This contradiction is best exemplified by the two-sided pressure the USA was exerting on Serbia in summer 2003: US representatives simultaneously demanded of the Serbian government that it deliver suspected war criminals to the International Criminal Court at The Hague (in accordance with the logic of the global Empire which demands a trans-state global judicial institution) *and* that it sign a bilateral treaty with the USA prohibiting Serbia from ever delivering to any international institution (that is, to the *same* Hague Court) any US citizen suspected of war crimes or other crimes against humanity (in accordance with nation-state logic) – no wonder the Serb reaction was one of perplexed fury.[3] The same goes for Croatia: the USA is now exerting tremendous pressure on the Croat government to extradite a couple of its generals accused of war crimes during the struggles in Bosnia to the Hague Court. The reaction is, of course: how can they ask this of *us*, when *they* do not recognize the legitimacy of the Hague Court? Or are American citizens, in effect, 'more equal than others'? If one simply universalizes the underlying principles of the Bush doctrine, would not India be fully justified in attacking Pakistan? Pakistan does indeed directly harbour and support anti-Indian terrorists in Kashmir, and it possesses (nuclear) weapons of mass destruction – not to mention China's right to attack Taiwan, and so on, with all the consequences that might entail.

The first permanent global war crimes court (the ICC) started work on 1 July 2002 in The Hague, with the power to tackle genocide, crimes against humanity, and war crimes. Anyone, from a head of state to an ordinary citizen, will be liable to ICC prosecution for human rights violations, including systematic murder, torture, rape and sexual slavery. Or, as Kofi Annan put it: 'There must be a recognition that we are all members of one human family. We have to create new institutions. This is one of them. This is another step forward in humanity's slow march toward civilization.' However, while human rights groups have hailed the Court's creation as the biggest milestone for international justice since the trial of leading Nazis by an international military tribunal in Nuremberg after World War II, the Court faces stiff opposition from the United States, Russia and China. The United States claims that the Court will infringe national sovereignty, and could lead to politically motivated prosecutions of its officials or soldiers working outside US borders; the US Congress is even considering legislation authorizing US forces to invade The Hague, in the event that prosecutors grab a US national. The noteworthy paradox here is that the USA thus rejects the jurisdiction of a tribunal which was constituted with the full support (and vote) of the USA itself!

The same logic of exception also applies to economic relations. On 21 December 2002, the BBC reported that the 'US Blocks Cheap Drugs Agreement':

> The United States has blocked an international agreement to allow poor countries to buy cheap drugs. This means millions of poor people will still not have access to medicines for diseases such as HIV/AIDS, malaria and tuberculosis. 'One hundred and forty-three countries stood on the same ground, we were hoping to make that unanimous.' The principle of allowing developing countries access to cheap versions of

drugs still protected by copyright had been agreed at WTO talks a year ago.

The same story repeated itself in Cancún in September 2003, when the USA insisted on subsidies for cotton farmers, thus violating its own sacrosanct advice to Third World countries to suspend state subsidies and open themselves up to the market.

And does the same not hold even for torture? The exemplary economic strategy of today's capitalism is outsourcing – giving over the 'dirty' process of material production (but also publicity, design, accountancy . . .) to another company via subcontracting. In this way, one can easily evade ecological and health rules: the production is done in, say, Indonesia, where the ecological and health regulations are much more lax than in the West, and the Western global company which owns the logo can claim that it is not responsible for the violations of another company. Are we not getting something homologous with regard to torture? Is not torture also being 'outsourced', left to Third World allies of the USA which can do it without worrying about legal problems or public protest? Was not such outsourcing explicitly advocated by Jonathan Alter in *Newsweek* immediately after 9/11? After stating: 'We can't legalize torture; it's contrary to American values', he none the less concludes that 'we'll have to think about transferring some suspects to our less squeamish allies, even if that's hypocritical. Nobody said this was going to be pretty.' This is how, today, First World democracy increasingly functions: by 'outsourcing' its dirty underside to other countries.

This inconsistency has deep geopolitical roots. Countries such as Saudi Arabia and Kuwait are deeply conservative monarchies but economic allies of America, fully integrated into Western capitalism. Here, the USA has a very precise and simple interest: if these countries are to be relied on for their oil reserves, *they have to remain non-democratic*. That is to say: it is a safe bet that democratic elections in Saudi Arabia or Iraq would bring to power a pro-Islamic nationalist regime riding on anti-American popular feeling. We therefore know now what 'bringing democracy' means: the USA and its 'willing partners' impose themselves as the ultimate judges as to whether a country is ripe for democracy – along these lines, Rumsfeld stated in April 2003 that Iraq should become not a 'theocracy' but a tolerant secular country in which all religions and ethnic groups would enjoy the same rights. Along the same lines, in October 2003, US representatives made it clear that any official recognition of the privileged position of Islam in the new Iraqi constitution would be unacceptable. The irony here is double: not only would it be nice if the USA were to demand the same from Israel with regard to Judaism, but it was precisely Saddam's Iraq which officially *already was a secular state*, while the result of democratic elections would be the privileging of Islam! In the same spirit, an unnamed senior US figure stated that 'the first foreign policy gesture of a democratic Iraq would be to recognize Israel'.[4]

Europe, Old and New

The only good argument for the war against Iraq was the one repeatedly made by Christopher Hitchens: we should not forget that the majority of Iraqis were effectively Saddam's victims, and that they would be really glad to get rid of him.[5] He was such a catastrophe for his country that an American occupation in *whatever* form might seem a much brighter prospect in terms of day-to-day survival and overall levels of terror. We are not talking here about 'bringing Western democracy to Iraq', simply about getting rid of the nightmare called Saddam. To these Iraqis, the caution expressed by Western liberals could not but appear deeply hypocritical – do they really care about how the Iraqi people feel?

One can make a more general point here: what about pro-Castro Western leftists who despise what the Cubans themselves call '*gusanos* [worms]', namely, the emigrants? But, with all due sympathy for the Cuban revolution, what right does a typical middle-class Western leftist have to despise a Cuban who decided to leave Cuba not only because of political disenchantment, but also because of poverty (so severe as to involve genuine hunger)? In the same vein, I myself remember dozens of Western leftists in the early 1990s who proudly pronounced that, for them, Yugoslavia still existed, and reproached me for betraying the unique chance of maintaining a united Yugoslavia – to which I always answered that I was not yet ready to lead my life so that it would not shatter the dreams of Western leftists. There are few things more worthy of contempt, few attitudes more *ideological* (if this word has any meaning today, it should be applied here), than a tenured Western academic leftist arrogantly dismissing (or, even worse, 'understanding' in a patronizing way) an Eastern European from a Communist country who longs for Western liberal democracy and some consumer goods. However, it is all too easy to slip from this to the notion that 'underneath, the Iraqis are just like us, and really want the same things we do'. The old story will repeat itself: America brings new hope and democracy to the people, but, instead of hailing the US army, the same ungrateful people reject it – they look the proverbial gift horse in the mouth, and America then reacts like a child with hurt feelings against the ingratitude of those it selflessly helped.

The underlying presupposition is the old one: if we scratch the surface, we are all Americans. That is our true desire – so all that is necessary is just to give people a chance, liberate them from their imposed constraints, and they will join us in our ideological dream. No wonder that, in February 2003, an American representative used the word 'capitalist revolution' to describe what the Americans are now doing: exporting their revolution around the entire world. No wonder they moved from 'containing' the enemy to a more aggressive stance. It is the USA which is now, as the defunct USSR was decades ago, the subversive agent of a world revolution. When Bush said recently, 'Freedom is not America's gift to other nations, it is God's gift to humanity', this apparent modesty none the less, in the best totalitarian fashion, conceals its very opposite. Recall the standard claim of a totalitarian leader that, in himself, he is nothing at all – his strength is only the strength of the people who stand behind him, he only expresses their deepest strivings; the catch, of course, is that, in this case, those who oppose the leader do not only oppose him, they also oppose the deepest and noblest aspirations of the people. . . . And does the same not hold for Bush's claim? If freedom were in fact just America's gift to other nations, things would have been much easier – those who opposed US policies would be doing just that, opposing the politics of the USA as a single nation-state. However, if freedom is God's gift to humanity (and

– this is the hidden proviso – if the USA perceives itself as the chosen instrument for distributing this gift to all the nations of the world), then those who oppose US policies are *eo ipso* rejecting God's noblest gift to humanity. It is no surprise that many authentic theologians are appalled by such statements by Bush, detecting in them a terrifying sacrilege.

Nevertheless, there is a grain of truth in Rumsfeld's ironic reference to the 'old Europe'. The united Franco–German stand against the US policy on Iraq should be read against the background of the Franco–German summit in autumn 2003, at which Chirac and Schröder basically proposed a kind of dual Franco–German hegemony over the European Community. So no wonder anti-Americanism is at its strongest in 'big' European nations, especially France and Germany: it is part of their resistance to globalization. We often hear the complaint that the recent trend of globalization threatens the sovereignty of the nation-states; here, however, one should qualify this statement: *which* states are most exposed to this threat? It is not the small states, but the second-rank (ex-)world powers, countries like the United Kingdom, Germany and France: what they fear is that, once they are fully immersed in the newly emerging global Empire, they will be reduced to the same level as, say, Austria, Belgium, or even Luxembourg. The refusal of 'Americanization' in France, shared by many leftists and rightist nationalists, is thus ultimately the refusal to accept the fact that France itself is losing its hegemonic role in Europe. The levelling of influence between larger and smaller nation-states should thus be counted among the beneficial effects of globalization: beneath the derision for the new Eastern European post-Communist states, it is easy to discern the contours of the wounded narcissism of the European 'great nations'. And this great-state-nationalism is not just a feature external to the (failure of) the present opposition; it affects the very way France and Germany articulated this opposition. Instead of doing, even more actively, precisely what the Americans were doing – *mobilizing* the 'new European' states on their own politico-military platform, *organizing* the new common front – France and Germany arrogantly acted alone.

In the French resistance against the war on Iraq, there is definitely a clear echo of the 'old decadent' Europe: escape the problem by inaction, by new resolutions upon old resolutions – all this is reminiscent of the inactivity of the League of Nations against Germany in the 1930s. And the pacifist call of 'let the inspectors do their work' clearly *was* hypocritical: they were allowed to do their work only because there was a credible threat of military intervention. And all this is not even to mention French neo-colonialism in Africa (from Congo-Brazzaville to the sinister French role in the Rwanda massacres). Need we add the French role in the Bosnian war? And is it not significant how, immediately after the start of the Iraqi war, the same European countries which opposed it (France and Germany) adopted the attitude of 'OK, now that the war is here, let's go on to the next topic, the postwar reconstruction of Iraq' – thus delivering the message 'We did our formal duty and protested, now let's get back to business as usual!'[6]

A Tale of Heroes and Cowards

The war on Iraq can be seen as the moment of truth when the 'official' political distinctions are blurred. Generally, we live in a topsy-turvy world in which Republicans spend money freely, creating record budget deficits, while Democrats maintain a balanced budget; in which Republicans, who thunder against big government and preach the devolution of power to states and local communities, are in the process of creating the strongest state mechanism of control in the entire history of humanity. The same applies to the post-Communist countries. A good example is the case of Poland: the most ardent supporter of US policies in Poland is the ex-Communist President Kwasniewski (who is even tipped as the future head of NATO, after George Robertson), while the main opposition to Poland's participation in the anti-Iraq coalition comes from the rightist parties. Towards the end of January 2003, the Polish bishops also demanded from the government that it should add to the contract which regulates Poland's membership in the EU a special paragraph guaranteeing that Poland will 'retain the right to keep its fundamental values as they are formulated in its constitution' – by which, of course, are meant the prohibition of abortion, of euthanasia and of same-sex marriages.

The very ex-Communist countries which are the most ardent supporters of the US 'war on terror' are profoundly concerned that their cultural identity, their very survival as nations, is threatened by the onslaught of cultural 'Americanization' as the price for their immersion in global capitalism – thus we are witnessing the paradox of pro-Bushist anti-Americanism. In Slovenia, my own country, there is a similar inconsistency: rightist nationalists criticize the ruling Centre–Left coalition for the fact that although it is publicly for joining NATO and supporting the US anti-terrorist campaign, it is secretly sabotaging it, participating in it for opportunist reasons, not out of conviction. At the same time, however, they accuse the coalition of wanting to undermine Slovene national identity by advocating full integration into Westernized global capitalism, and thus drowning Slovenes in contemporary Americanized pop culture. The idea is that the ruling coalition sustains pop culture, stupid TV programmes, mindless consumption, and all the rest, in order to turn the Slovenes into an easily manipulated mass, incapable of serious reflection and a firm ethical stance. In short, the underlying logic is that the ruling coalition stands for the 'liberal–Communist plot': ruthless unconstrained immersion in global capitalism is perceived as the latest dark plot of the ex-Communists, enabling them to retain their secret hold on power.

Thus the almost tragic misunderstanding resides in the fact that the nationalists, on the one hand, unconditionally support NATO (under US command), accusing the ruling coalition of secretly supporting anti-globalists and anti-American pacifists, while, on the other hand, they worry about the fate of Slovene identity in the globalization process, claiming that the ruling coalition wants to throw Slovenia into the global whirlpool, without a thought for national identity. Ironically, the new emerging socio-ideological order these nationalist conservatives are bemoaning reads like what the New Left, back in the 1960s, criticized as capitalist 'repressive tolerance', in which freedom and unfreedom strangely overlap: what looks like 'freedom' is in fact 'unfreedom' itself.

If there is an ethical hero of recent times in ex-Yugoslavia, it is Ika Sarič, a modest judge in Croatia who – without any clear public support, and despite threats to her own life – condemned General Mirko Norac and his colleagues to twelve years in prison for crimes committed in 1992 against the Serb civilian population. Even the leftist government, afraid of the threat of rightist nationalist demonstrations, refused to stand firmly behind the trial against Norac. However, when the sentence was proclaimed, during a feverish phase characterized by threats from the nationalist Right of large-scale public disorder to topple the government, *nothing happened*: the demonstrations were much smaller than expected, and Croatia 'rediscovered' itself as a state under the rule of law. It was especially important that Norac was not delivered to The Hague, but condemned in Croatia itself – thus Croatia proved that it does not need international tutelage. The true dimension of the act proper consisted in the shift from the impossible to the possible: before the sentence, the nationalist Right, with its veteran organizations, was perceived as a powerful force not to be provoked, and the direct harsh sentence was perceived by the liberal Left as something which 'we all want, but, unfortunately, cannot afford at this difficult moment, since chaos would ensue' – after the sentence was proclaimed, however, as I have said, nothing happened: the impossible turned into the routine. If there is still any dimension to be redeemed of the signifier 'Europe', then this act was 'European' in the most pathetic sense of the term.

And if there is one event which embodies cowardice, it is the behaviour of the Slovene government after the outbreak of the Iraq–US War. Slovene politicians desperately tried to steer a middle course between US pressure and the unpopularity of the war with the majority of the Slovene population. First, Slovenia signed the infamous Vilnius Declaration, for which it was praised by Rumsfeld and others as part of the 'new Europe', of the 'coalition of the willing' in the war against Iraq. After the Foreign Minister signed the document, however, there ensued a true comedy of denials: the minister claimed that, before signing the document, he had consulted the president of the republic and other dignitaries, who promptly denied that they knew anything about it; then, all concerned claimed that the document did not in any way support the unilateral US attack on Iraq, but called for a key role for the UN. The specification was that Slovenia supported the disarmament of Iraq, not the war on Iraq. A couple of days later, however, there was a nasty surprise from the USA: Slovenia was not only explicitly named among the countries who participated in the 'coalition of the willing', but was even designated as the recipient of financial aid from the USA to its war partners. What ensued was truly farcical: Slovenia proudly declared that it was not participating in the war against Iraq, and demanded to be struck off the list. After a couple of days, a new embarrassing document was received: the USA officially thanked Slovenia for its support and help. Slovenia again protested that it did not qualify for any gratitude; it refused to recognize itself as the proper addressee of the letter of thanks, in a kind of mocking version of 'Please, I don't really deserve your thanks!', as if sending its thanks was the worst thing the USA could do to us right now. Usually, states protest when they are unjustly criticized; Slovenia protests when it receives signs of gratitude. In short, Slovenia behaved as if it were not the proper recipient of the letters of praise, which went on and on — and what we all knew was that, in this case also, the letter *did* arrive at its destination.

Was will Europa?

Late in his life, Freud asked the famous question '*Was will das Weib?*', admitting his perplexity in the face of the enigma of feminine sexuality. And a similar perplexity is aroused when one tries to define the contours of a 'Europe' to be defended. Which Europe?

In the trans-European philosophico-political media offensive instigated in summer 2003 by Jürgen Habermas and Jacques Derrida, a series of philosophers argued that, faced with the challenge of the new American Empire, Europe should find the strength to reassert its ethico-political legacy. When we encounter such accord between philosophers whose thought is otherwise incompatible, we should immediately become suspicious: what does such a call amount to politically, beyond vague unease and resistance to the ever stronger hegemony of the USA? If it is only a *reaction* to this threat made on behalf of what seems to be threatened by it — a plea for a little more 'radical' democracy, human rights, tolerance, solidarity, welfare state — this is clearly not enough.

For many years, I have pleaded for a renewed 'leftist Euro-centrism'. To put it bluntly: do we want to live in a world in which the only choice is between the American civilization and the emerging Chinese authoritarian-capitalist one? If the answer is no, then the true alternative is Europe. The Third World cannot generate a strong enough resistance to the ideology of the American Dream; in the present constellation, only Europe can do that. The true opposition today is not between the First World and the Third World, but between the ensemble of First and Third Worlds (the American global Empire and its colonies) and the remaining Second World (Europe). Apropos of Freud, Theodor Adorno claimed that what we observe in the contemporary 'verwaltete Welt' and its 'repressive desublimation' is no longer the old logic of repression of *das Es* and its *Triebe*, but a perverse direct pact between *das Überich* (social authority) and *das Es* (illicit aggressive drives) at the expense of *das Ich*. Something structurally similar seems to be occurring today at the political level: a weird pact between postmodern global capitalism and premodern societies, at the expense of modernity proper. It is easy for the American multiculturalist global Empire to integrate premodern local traditions – the foreign body which it cannot actually assimilate is European modernity. Jihad and McWorld are two sides of the same coin; Jihad is already McJihad.

Although the ongoing 'war on terror' presents itself as the defence of the democratic legacy, it courts the danger clearly perceived a century ago by G.K. Chesterton who, in *Orthodoxy*, laid bare the fundamental deadlock of the critics of religion:

> Men who begin to fight the Church for the sake of freedom and humanity end by flinging away freedom and humanity if only they may fight the Church. . . . The secularists have not wrecked divine things; but the secularists have wrecked secular things, if that is any comfort to them.[7]

Does the same not hold today for advocates of religion themselves? How many fanatical defenders of religion started by ferociously attacking contemporary secular culture, and ended up forsaking any meaningful religious experience? In a similar way, many liberal warriors are so eager to fight anti-democratic fundamentalism that they will end up by flinging away freedom and democracy themselves. They have such a passion for proving that non-Christian fundamentalism is the main threat to freedom that they are ready to fall back on the position that we have to limit our own freedom here and now, in our allegedly Christian societies. If the 'terrorists' are ready to wreck this world for love of another world, our warriors on terror are ready to wreck their own democratic world out of hatred for the Muslim other. Some of them love human dignity so much that they are ready to legalize torture – the ultimate degradation of human dignity – to defend it. . . .

Along the same lines, the properly dialectical paradox is that we may lose 'Europe' through its very defence. Recently, an ominous decision of the European Union passed almost unnoticed: the plan to establish an all-European border police force to secure the isolation of Union territory, and thus to prevent the influx of immigrants. *This* is the truth of globalization: the construction of new walls safeguarding prosperous Europe from the immigrant hordes. Here I am inclined to bring in the old Marxist 'humanist' opposition of 'relations between things' and 'relations between persons': in the much-celebrated free circulation opened up by global capitalism, it is 'things' (commodities) which circulate freely, while the circulation of 'persons' is more and more controlled. This new racism of the developed world is, in a way, much more brutal than the previous form: its implicit legitimization is neither naturalist (the 'natural' superiority of the developed West) nor any longer culturalist (we in the West also want to preserve our cultural identity), but unabashed economic egotism – the fundamental divide is the one between those who are included in the sphere of (relative) economic prosperity and those who are excluded from it.

Two conclusions impose themselves. If the European legacy is to be effectively defended, then the first move should be a thorough self-criticism. What we find reprehensible and dangerous in US policies and civilization is *a part of Europe itself*, one of the possible outcomes of the European project – so there is no room for self-satisfied arrogance. The USA is a distorted mirror of Europe itself. Back in the 1930s, Max Horkheimer wrote that those who do not want to speak (critically) about liberalism should also keep silent about Fascism. *Mutatis mutandis*, one should say to those who attack the new imperialism of the USA: those who do not want to engage critically with Europe itself should also keep silent about the USA.

This brings us to the key dilemma. If the defence of the European legacy limits itself to the defence of the threatened European democratic tradition of solidarity and human rights, the battle is lost in advance. If the European legacy is to be defended, Europe has to *reinvent* itself: in the act of defence, one has to reinvent that which is to be defended. What we need is a ruthless questioning of the very foundations of the European legacy, up to and including those sacred cows, democracy and human rights. And, unfortunately, the philosophers' call for the defence of Europe falls somewhat short of this urgent task.

Everybody has been complaining recently that the European stand against the USA was weak and inconsistent, that Europe failed to assert itself as an autonomous political agent – however, is this very overwhelming awareness of failure not in itself a positive sign? Does it not, in a negative way, bear witness to the fact that Europe clearly perceives the need to assert itself, that it perceives the lack of such self-assertion as a failure? The lesson of feminism is instructive here: the first step for women was not to fight patriarchy, but to experience their situation as unjust and humiliating, and their passivity as a failure to act.

Here, I would like to propose the hypothesis that the US–Iraq war was, in terms of its actual sociopolitical content, *the first war between the USA and Europe*. That is to say: what if, as some economists have already suggested, the true economic aim of the war was not primarily the control of oil resources but the strengthening of the US dollar, the prevention of the dollar's defeat against the euro, the prevention of the collapse of a dollar which is less and less 'covered' by 'real' value (think of the immense US debt)? Today, a united Europe is the main obstacle to the New World Order the USA wants to impose.

A Modest Proposal for an Act in the Middle East

Another reason evoked by supporters of the attack on Iraq was that it would give a new impetus to the stalled Middle East peace process. Did it? The first thing to do as far as the Middle East is concerned is to abandon any notion that the crisis involves the geographical reality of the meagre land resources.

One cannot simply oppose plenitude (an excessive gift as an

expression of pure love, enough for one and all) and scarcity, with its selective 'economizing' attitude (there is not enough for everyone, so some have access while others do not), since excess itself has to be grounded in scarcity. In other words, scarcity (the idea of something lacking, of there being 'not enough for everyone') is not a simple fact, but a structural necessity: before being a lack of something specific, it is a purely formal lack, a lack which emerges at its frustratingly purest precisely when our needs are excessively fulfilled (remember Freud's case of the merry butcher's wife). Along the same lines, the possibility of the three most interesting deadly sins, envy, avarice and melancholy, is inscribed into the very formal structure of desire: a melancholic is unable to sustain desire in the presence of its object; a miser clings to the object, unable to consume it; an envious subject desires the object of another's desire. So either the other man's grass is by definition always greener than mine; or I just admire my own green grass in awe, unable to let my animals eat it; or I just gaze at it with the sad indifference of a melancholic. These paradoxes account for the truth of stories such as the one about the farmer to whom an angel appeared and told him: 'I will grant you a wish, whatever you want – only, beware, I will do twice as much to your neighbour!' The farmer replied, with an evil smile: 'Take one of my eyes!' Or the story about the poor peasant couple who sabotaged their chance of plenitude – when a fairy offered to grant them three wishes, the husband quickly blurted out: 'A sausage on my plate!' The angry wife snapped back: 'You fool – may the sausage stick to your nose!' So the final wish could only be a modest: 'May the sausage return from the nose to the plate!'

One has to be honest enough here to recognize the selective symbolic nature of suffering elevated to an exemplary status: what is the suffering of the Palestinians in the West Bank compared to the suffering of individuals in some backward Muslim states? What was the suffering of the Chileans under Pinochet compared to, say, the suffering in North Korea? (On the other hand, is the suffering of the Cubans really greater than the suffering of the dispossessed crowds in the non-Communist Latin American countries? Not to mention the unimaginable protracted nightmare going on in the Congo or Liberia. . . .) In this simpl(ifi)e(d) sense, it is indeed unfair to elevate the Palestinians into the global symbol of suffering – were their situation really so desperate, they would have emigrated *en masse* to Jordan and other relatively prosperous Arab countries. It is as if there is in the critique of the policies of the State of Israel an element of – not so much 'unfair' anti-Semitism but, rather, on the contrary – secret recognition of the special higher ethical standards of the Jews: how can *you*, of all peoples, behave like this?

The great mystery apropos of the Israeli–Palestinian conflict is: *why does it persist for so long, when everybody knows the only viable solution* – an Israeli withdrawal from the West Bank and Gaza, the establishment of a Palestinian state, the renunciation by the Palestinians of their refugees' right to return to the land within the borders of pre-1967 Israel, as well as some kind of a compromise over Jerusalem? Whenever agreement seemed to be at hand, it inexplicably disappeared. How often does it happen that, when peace seems to be simply a matter of finding a proper formulation for some minor statements, everything suddenly falls apart, displaying the frailty of the negotiated compromise? There is in fact something of a neurotic symptom in the Middle Eastern conflict – everyone recognizes the way to get rid of the obstacle, yet, none the less, no one wants to remove it, as if there is some kind of pathological libidinal profit gained by persisting in the deadlock.

I am tempted to call this a symptomal *knot*: is it not that, in the Israeli–Palestinian conflict, the standard roles are somehow reversed, twisted around as in a knot? Israel – officially representing Western liberal modernity in the area – legitimizes itself in terms of its ethnic-religious identity, while the Palestinians – decried as premodern 'fundamentalists' – legitimize their demands in terms of secular citizenship. So we have the paradox of the State of Israel, the supposed island of liberal democratic modernity in the Middle East, countering Arab demands with an even more 'fundamentalist' ethno-religious claim to its sacred land.

And, as the story of the Gordian knot tells us, the only way to resolve such a deadlock is not to unravel the knot, but to cut it. Rabin took the first big step in this direction when he recognized the PLO as the legitimate representative of the Palestinians, and thus as the only true partner in negotiations. When Rabin announced the reversal of the Israeli policy of 'no negotiations with the PLO, a terrorist organization', and pronounced the simple words 'Let us end this charade [of negotiating with the Palestinians with no public links to the PLO] and start talking to our real partners', the situation changed overnight. That is the effect of a true political act: it changes the co-ordinates of the situation, and renders the unthinkable thinkable. Rabin's military past was at once relegated as less important – he became the man who recognized the PLO as a legitimate partner. Although he was a Labour politician, Rabin thus accomplished a gesture that characterizes conservative politicians at their best. The Israeli elections of 28 January 2003 were, on the contrary, the clearest indicator of the failure of modern conservatives, of their inability to perform historical acts in the spirit of Charles de Gaulle, or even Richard Nixon. Only a De Gaulle could have granted Algeria independence; only a conservative such as Nixon could have established relations with China. Along the same lines, 70 per cent of Israelis know that the proposal of the Labour candidate Amram Mitzma – Israel's unconditional withdrawal from the West Bank and Gaza – is the only solution to the crisis. However, since Mitzma is a decent ethical figure, with no 'strong-man' charisma, they do not trust him to be able to accomplish this act. What is therefore needed is (in the tradition of Rabin) a figure such as Sharon to take Mitzma's programme on board – which, of course, Sharon is manifestly unable to do.

The underlying problem is not only that the Arabs do not really accept the existence of the State of Israel – the Israeli Jews themselves also do not really accept the Palestinian presence on the West Bank. We all know Bertolt Brecht's *boutade* apropos of the East Berlin workers' uprising in July 1953: 'The Party is not satisfied with its people, so it will replace them with a new people more supportive of its politics.' Is not something homologous discernible today in the relationship between the State of Israel and the Palestinians? The Israeli state is not comfortable with the people on the West Bank and in Gaza, so it considers the option of replacing them with another people. That it is, precisely, the Jews, the exemplary victims, who are now considering a radical 'ethnic cleansing' (the 'transfer' – a perfect Orwellian misnomer

– of the Palestinians from the West Bank) is the ultimate paradox demanding closer consideration.

If there was ever a passionate attachment to the lost object, a refusal to come to terms with its loss, it is the Jewish attachment to their land and Jerusalem, the '[See you] next year in Jerusalem!' And are the present troubles not the supreme proof of the catastrophic consequences of such a radical fidelity, when it is taken literally? Over the last two thousand years, when the Jews were fundamentally a nation without land, living permanently in exile, with no firm roots in their places of residence, their reference to Jerusalem was, fundamentally, a purely negative one, a prohibition against 'painting an image of home', against feeling at home anywhere on earth. However, with the process of returning to Palestine, which started a century ago, the metaphysical Other Place was directly identified with a determinate place on earth. When the Jews lost their land and elevated it into the mythical lost object, 'Jerusalem' became much more than a piece of land: it became the metaphor for the coming of the Messiah, for a metaphysical home, for the end of the wandering which characterizes human existence. The mechanism is well known: after an object is lost, it becomes a stand-in for much more, for all that we miss in our earthly lives. *When a thousand-year-old dream is finally close to realization, such a realization can only turn into a nightmare.*

According to Jewish tradition, Lilith is the woman a man makes love to while he masturbates alone in his bed during the night[8] – so, far from standing for feminine identity liberated from the grip of patriarchy, as some feminists claim, her status is purely phallic: she is what Lacan calls *La femme*, the Woman, the phantasmatic supplement of male masturbatory phallic *jouissance*. Significantly, while there is only one man (Adam), femininity is from the very beginning split between Eve and Lilith, between the 'ordinary' hysterical barred subject ($) and the phantasmatic spectre of Woman: when a man is having sex with a 'real' woman, he is using her as a masturbatory prop to support his fantasies about the nonexistent Woman. . . .[9] The catastrophe occurs when the two women collapse into one, when the 'ordinary' partner is elevated to the dignity of Lilith – which is structurally perfectly homo-logous to the Zionist elevation of the 'ordinary' Jerusalem into the Jerusalem the Jews had been dreaming about for thousands of years. . . . .

Thus the ethical choice is ultimately a simple one: the only true fidelity to the memory of the Holocaust lies in recognition of the injustice committed against the Palestinians; any justification of current Israeli policies by reference to the Holocaust is the worst possible ethical betrayal. It is therefore easy to answer the big question: what would be the truly radical ethico-political act today in the Middle East? For both Israelis and Arabs, it would consist in the gesture of renouncing (political) control of Jer-usalem – that is, of endorsing the transformation of the Old Town of Jerusalem into an extra-statal place of religious worship con-trolled (temporarily) by some neutral international force. What both sides should accept is that, by renouncing political control of Jerusalem, they would, in effect, be renouncing nothing – they would be *gaining* the elevation of Jerusalem into a genuinely extra-political, sacred site. What they would lose is, precisely and only, what already, in itself, *deserves* to be lost: the reduction of religion to a bargaining chip in political power conflicts.

One should not renounce the 'impossible' dream of a bi-national secular state bringing together the Israeli Jews and the Palestinians. In the long term, the true utopia is not that of this bi-national state, but that of the wall clearly separating the two communities. Pictures of the wall that separates pre-1967 Israel from the West Bank's occupied territories reveal an uncanny resemblance to the wall that separated East Germany from West Germany until 1989. The illusion of this new wall is that it will serve as the demarcation line separating the 'normal' rule of law and social life from the permanent state of emergency – that it will confine the state of emergency to the domain 'out there'. In order for there to be another true event in the Middle East – the explosion of true political universality in the Pauline sense of 'for us there are no Jews and no Palestinians' – each of the two sides would have to realize that this renunciation of the ethnically 'clean' nation-state is a liberation for themselves, not only a sacrifice to be made for the other. The paradox is thus that, in the entire Middle East, the Palestinians, these 'Jews among/of the Arabs', are, because of their unique position, the only collective agent upon whom the role of the modernizer, capable of moving to a political form beyond ethnic identity, is imposed: the only true long-term solution to the Middle Eastern crisis is the emergence of Palestinians as political modernizers.

The Achilles heel of non-Zionist liberal Jews is best encapsulated by their standard argument: 'OK, of course we should negotiate, accept the Palestinian state, the end of occupation, even the prospect of a single bi-national secular state – but in order for serious talks to start, the senseless suicide bombing terror has to stop, one simply cannot engage in a dialogue under

such circumstances.' Horror at the 'irrational' excess of suicide
bombings, pure expenditure, the non-negotiable. . . . What is
really at stake here, however, is the return to normality: were the
'terrorists' to stop their acts, and thus ease the pressure, we
would be able to relax, breathe easily – and go on as normal.
Élisabeth Roudinesco writes:

> For now, the only apocalypse that seems to threaten Western
> society – and Islam as well – is radical Islamic fundament-
> alism disposed to terrorism. Islamic threats are made by
> extremist bearded and barbaric polygamists who constrain
> women's bodies and spit invectives against homosexuals,
> whom they hold responsible for weakening the masculine
> values of God the father.[10]

What makes this statement problematic is not only its very
'politically correct' distinction between Islamic fundamentalism
and Islam as such, which is also threatened by the former – in the
same way, Bush, Blair and even Sharon never forget to praise
Islam as a great religion of love and tolerance which has nothing
to do with disgusting terrorist acts. Neither is the problem the use
of the term 'radical Islamic fundamentalism disposed to terrorism' (or 'Islamic threats'). As Alain Badiou points out:

> when a predicate is attributed to a *formal* substance (as is the
> case with any derivation of a substantive from a formal
> adjective) it has no other consistency than that of giving an
> ostensible content to that form. In 'Islamic terrorism', the
> predicate 'Islamic' has no other function except that of

supplying an apparent content to the word 'terrorism' which is itself devoid of all content (in this instance, political).[11]

To put it in Kantian terms: the predicate 'Islamic' provides a fake 'schematization' of the purely formal category 'terrorism', conferring on it a false substantial density. To put it in Hegelese: the truth of such a *reflexive determination* ('Islamic terror') is its inherent and unavoidable reversal into *determinate reflection*: 'terrorist Islam', that is, terrorism as constitutive of the very *identity* of Islam.[12] The thing that makes Roudinesco's statement truly problematic, however, is that it endorses the aforementioned liberal logic which elevates the rejection of terrorism into a kind of transcendental a priori: first *that*, and only then can we negotiate . . . (or, to put it in Ernesto Laclau's terms, 'terrorism' has to be *excluded* so that the agonism of the democratic political struggle can take place). What is foreclosed in this way is the thematic presentation of (and confrontation with) 'terrorism' as (part of) a *political project*, which, of course, in no way implies the agreement with it. Here it is worth recalling Ernst Nolte's book on Heidegger, which brought a breath of fresh air into the eternal debate on 'Heidegger and the political' on account of its 'unacceptable' option: far from excusing Heidegger's infamous political choice in 1933, it justified it − or, at least, it de-demonized it, presenting it as a viable and meaningful choice. Against the standard defenders of Heidegger, whose mantra is that Heidegger's Nazi engagement was a personal mistake with no fundamental consequences for his thought, Nolte accepted the basic claim of Heidegger's critics that his Nazi choice is inscribed in his thought − but with a twist: instead of problematizing his thought, Nolte justified his political choice as a viable option in the situation of the late 1920s and early 1930s in the context of economic chaos and the Communist threat:

> In so far as Heidegger resisted the attempt at the [Communist] solution, he, like countless others, was historically right. . . . In committing himself to the [National Socialist] solution perhaps he became a 'fascist'. But in no way did that make him historically wrong from the outset.[13]

Nolte also formulated the basic terms and tropes of the 'revisionist' debate, whose fundamental tenet is to 'objectively compare' Fascism and Communism: Fascism, and even Nazism, was ultimately a reaction to the Communist threat and a repetition of its worst practices (concentration camps, mass liquidations of political enemies):

> Could it be the case that the National Socialists and Hitler carried out an 'Asiatic' deed [the Holocaust] only because they considered themselves and their kind to be potential or actual victims of a [Bolshevik] 'Asiatic' deed? Did not the 'Gulag Archipelago' precede Auschwitz?[14]

Nolte's strong point is his serious approach to the task of grasping Fascism – and even Nazism – as a feasible political project, which is a *sine qua non* for its effective criticism. This is where one has to make the choice: the 'pure' liberal stance of equidistance towards leftist and rightist 'totalitarianism' (both are evil, based on the intolerance of political and other differences, the rejection of democratic and humanist values, etc.) is a priori false. One *has* to take sides and proclaim that one is fundamentally 'worse' than the other – for this reason, the ongoing 'relativization' of Fascism, the notion that one should compare the two totalitarianisms rationally, and so on, *always* involves the – explicit or implicit – thesis that Fascism was 'better' than Communism, an understandable reaction to the Communist threat.

In summer 2003, Silvio Berlusconi provoked a violent outcry with his statement that, while Mussolini was indeed a dictator, he was not a political criminal and murderer like Hitler, Stalin or Saddam – but we should bear in mind what was truly at stake in this scandal: far from deserving to be dismissed as Berlusconi's personal idiosyncrasy, his statement is part of a larger ongoing ideologico-political project of changing the terms of the post-World War II symbolic pact of European identity based on anti-Fascist unity. And do we not find the flip side to this rejection of thinking Nazism as a political project in the crucial theoretical scandal of Adorno (and the Frankfurt School in general): the total absence of any analysis of Stalinism (a lacuna reproduced in the work of Habermas and others). Perhaps that is the ultimate enigma of the tension between Adorno and Hannah Arendt: while they both shared a radical rejection of Stalinism, Arendt based it on the explicit large-scale analysis of the 'origins of totalitarianism', as well as on the positive normative notion of *vis activa*, of the engaged political life; while Adorno rejected this step.[15]

Just as the distinction between 'good' Islam and 'bad' Islamic terrorism is a fake, one should also see as problematic the typical 'radical-liberal' distinction between Jews and the State of Israel or Zionism – that is, the effort to open up a space in which Jews and

Jewish citizens of Israel would be able to criticize the State of Israel's politics and Zionist ideology not only without being accused of anti-Semitism, but, even more, by formulating their critique as based on their very passionate attachment to Jewishness, on what they see as worth saving in the Jewish legacy.[16] However, is this enough? Marx said of the petty bourgeois that he sees in every object two aspects, one bad and one good, and tries to keep the good and fight the bad. One should avoid the same mistake in dealing with Judaism: the 'good' Levinasian Judaism of justice, respect for and responsibility towards the other, and so on, against the 'bad' tradition of Jehovah, with His fits of vengeance and genocidal violence against the neighbouring people. This is the illusion to be avoided: one should assert a Hegelian 'speculative identity' between these two aspects, and see in Jehovah *support* for justice and responsibility. Judaism is, as such, the moment of unbearable absolute contradiction, the worst (monotheistic violence) and the best (responsibility towards the other) in an absolute tension: the same, coinciding, and simultaneously absolutely incompatible. In short, one should have the courage to transpose the gap, the tension, into the very core of Judaism: it is no longer a question of defending the pure Jewish tradition of justice and love for the neighbour against the Zionist aggressive assertion of the nation-state. And, along the same lines, instead of celebrating the greatness of true Islam against its misuse by fundamentalist terrorists, or bemoaning the fact that, of all the great religions, Islam is the most resistant to modernization, one should, rather, conceive of this resistance as an open chance, as 'undecidable': this resistance does not necessarily lead to 'Islamo-Fascism', it can also be articulated into a socialist project.

Precisely because Islam harbours the 'worst' potentials of the Fascist answer to our present predicament, it can also turn out to be the site for the 'best'. In other words, yes, Islam is indeed not a religion like the others, it does involve a stronger social link, it does resist integration into the capitalist global order – and the task is work out how to use this ambiguous fact politically.

In the case of Judaism as well as in the case of Islam, one should thus dare to accomplish the Hegelian step towards 'concrete universality', and to transpose the site of antagonism and inconsistency into the very core of the religious edifice, not to dismiss it as pertaining only to the secondary fundamentalist misuse. One myth to be dispelled is the one about secular Israeli 'liberals' fighting religious 'fundamentalists' – in short, cosmopolitan Tel Aviv society fighting the Jerusalem community. Such simple oppositions make it easy to forget some key facts: that Tel Aviv is, for all practical purposes, *judenfrei*, with practically no Palestinians; that some of the most ardent opponents of the Israeli occupation of the West Bank are the ultra-'fundamentalist' Jewish groups; that more new settlements were constructed under the 'doveish' Barak government than under the 'hawkish' Netanyahu government.

History confronts us with unexpected examples of what Deleuze called 'disjunctive synthesis', the co-dependence of radically exclusive positions. Anyone who is interested in the history of anti-Semitism should remember 26 September 1937: on that day, Adolf Eichmann and his assistant boarded a train in Berlin in order to visit Palestine: Heydrich himself gave Eichmann permission to accept the invitation of Feivel Polkes, a senior high member of Hagannah (the Zionist secret organization), to visit

Tel Aviv and discuss the co-ordination of German and Jewish organizations in order to facilitate the emigration of Jews to Palestine. Both the Germans and the Zionists wanted as many Jews as possible to move to Palestine. The Germans preferred to have them out of Western Europe, and the Zionists themselves wanted the Jews in Palestine to outnumber the Arabs as quickly as possible. (The visit failed because, due to some violent unrest, the British blocked the access to Palestine; but Eichmann and Polkes did meet days later in Cairo, and discussed the co-ordination of German and Zionist activities.)[17] Is not this weird incident the supreme example of how the Nazis and the radical Zionists shared a common interest? In both cases, the purpose was a kind of 'ethnic cleansing', that is, a violent change in the ratio of ethnic groups in the population.

The 'Silent Revolution'

Where, then, do we stand with reasons *pro et contra* the war? Abstract pacifism is intellectually stupid and morally wrong – one must stand firm against a threat. Of course the fall of Saddam is a relief to a large majority of the Iraqi people. Even more, of course, militant Islam is a horrifying reactionary ideology. Of course there is something hypocritical in all the reasons put forward against the war: the revolt should come from the Iraqi people themselves; we should not impose our values on them; war is never the answer, and so on. *But*, although all this is true, the attack was wrong – and it was *who did it* that made it wrong. The question should be: *who are you to do this?* The question is not one of war or peace, it is the well-founded 'gut feeling' that there was something terribly wrong with *this* war, that something will change irretrievably as a result of it.

One of Jacques Lacan's outrageous statements was that, even if what a jealous husband claims about his wife (that she sleeps around with other men) turns out to be true, his jealousy is still pathological. Along the same lines, one could say that even if most of the Nazi claims about the Jews had been true (that they exploited the Germans, that they seduced German girls, and so forth . . .), their anti-Semitism would still have been (and was) pathological, since it repressed the true reason why the Nazis *needed* anti-Semitism in order to sustain their ideological position. And the same should be said today apropos of the USA's claim that 'Saddam has weapons of mass destruction!' – even if this claim were to be true (and it probably is, at least to some extent), it is still false with regard to the position from which it is enunciated.

On 11 September 2001, the Twin Towers were struck. Twelve years earlier, on 9 November 1989, the Berlin Wall fell. That day, 9 November 1989, heralded the 'happy '90s', the Francis Fukuyama dream of the 'end of history', the belief that liberal democracy had, in principle, won, that the search was over, that the advent of a global, liberal world community lurked just around the corner, that the obstacles to this ultra-Hollywood happy ending were merely empirical and contingent (local pockets of resistance where the leaders had not yet grasped that their time was over). In contrast, 9/11 is the key symbol of the end of the Clintonite happy '90s, of the approaching era in which new walls emerge everywhere: between Israel and the West Bank, around the European Union, along the US–Mexican border. The prospect of a new global crisis is looming: economic crises, military and other catastrophes, states of emergency. . . . It was the very inflation of abstract ethical rhetoric in George W. Bush's public statements (of the type 'Does the world have the courage to act against Evil or not?') which revealed the utter *ethical* misery of the US position – the function of ethical reference here is purely mystificatory; it merely serves to mask the true political stakes, which are not difficult to discern.

The real dangers are thus the long-term ones. Are we aware that we are in the midst of a 'soft revolution', in the course of which the unwritten rules determining the most elementary international logic are changing? America scolded Gerhard Schröder, a democratically elected leader, for maintaining a stance supported by the great majority of his population (plus, according to the polls in mid-February 2003, by around 59 per cent of the US population itself – who opposed a strike against Iraq without UN support).[18] In a perverse rhetorical twist, when the pro-war leaders are confronted with the brutal fact that their policies are out of tune with the majority of their population, they make recourse to the commonplace wisdom that 'a true leader leads, he does not follow' – and this from leaders otherwise obsessed with opinion polls.

On 5 March 2003, on the 'Buchanan & Press' news show on NBC, they displayed, on the television screen, a photo of the recently captured Khalid Sheikh Mohammed, the 'third man of al-Qaeda' – a mean-faced man with a moustache, in an indeterminate nightgown-type prison uniform, half opened and with something like bruises faintly discernible (hints that he was already being tortured?). While Pat Buchanan's rapid voice was asking, 'Should this man, who knows all the names and all the detailed plans for future terrorist attacks on the USA, be tortured, so that we get all this out of him?', the horror of it was that the photo, in all its details, already suggested the answer. No wonder the response of the other commentators, and viewers' calls, was an overwhelming 'Yes!' – this makes one nostalgic for the good old days of the colonial war in Algeria, when the torture practised by the French Army was a dirty secret. In effect, was this not a fairly close realization of what George Orwell imagined in *Nineteen Eighty-four*, in his vision of 'hate sessions', where the citizens are shown photos of traitors, and are supposed to boo and yell at them? And the story goes on: a day later, on Fox TV, a commentator claimed that one is allowed to do whatever one wishes with this prisoner – not only deprive him of sleep, but break his fingers, and so forth – because he is 'a piece of human garbage with no rights whatsoever'. *This* is the true catastrophe: that such public statements are even possible today.

The analogy with the recent cases of paedophilia in the Catholic Church is instructive here. What makes these cases so disturbing is that they did not just happen in religious surroundings – these surroundings were part of them, directly mobilized as the instrument of seduction:

> . . . the seduction technique employs religion. Almost always some sort of prayer has been used as foreplay. The very places where the molestation occurs are redolent of religion – the sacristy, the confessional, the rectory, Catholic schools and clubs with sacred pictures on the walls . . . a conjunction of the overstrict sexual instruction of the Church (e.g., on

the mortal sinfulness of masturbation, even one occurrence of which can, if not confessed, send one to hell) and a guide who can free one of inexplicably dark teaching by inexplicably sacred exceptions. [The predator] uses religion to sanction what he is up to, even calling sex part of his priestly ministry.[19]

So religion is not invoked just in order to provide a *frisson* of the forbidden – that is, to heighten the pleasure by making sex an act of transgression; on the contrary, sex itself is presented in religious terms, as the religious cure for sin (masturbation). The paedophile priests were not liberals who seduced boys by claiming that gay sexuality was healthy and permissible – in a masterful use of the reversal Lacan called *point de capiton*, they first insisted that the confessed sin of a boy (masturbation) really was mortal, then offered gay acts (say, mutual masturbation) – in other words, what cannot but seem to be an even *worse* sin – as a 'healing' process. The key to it is this mysterious 'transubstantiation' by means of which the prohibiting Law which makes us feel guilty apropos of an ordinary sin is enacted in the guise of a much worse sin – as if, in a kind of Hegelian coincidence of opposites, the Law coincides with the greatest transgression. G.K. Chesterton asserted the truly subversive, even revolutionary, character of orthodoxy – in his famous 'Defense of Detective Stories', he observed how the detective story 'keeps in some sense before the mind the fact that civilization itself is the most sensational of departures and the most romantic of rebellions. . . . [The police romance] is based on the fact that morality is the most dark and daring of conspiracies.'[20] And does the same not hold for the paedophile priest? Does his presence not confirm that 'morality is the most dark and daring of conspiracies'?

Present-day US politics, in its inherent structure, is a kind of political equivalent to Catholic paedophilia. The problem of its new moral vigour is not just that morality is manipulatively exploited, but that it is directly mobilized; the problem with its appeal to democracy is not that it is simply hypocrisy and external manipulation, but that it directly mobilizes and relies on 'sincere' democratic aspirations.

The exemplary role of the 'war on terror' prisoners held in Guantánamo resides in the fact that their status is directly that of *Homo sacer*: there are no legal rules regulating their imprisonment; they find themselves literally in a legal void, reduced to basic subsistence. And is not the brutal intervention of the Russian police into the Moscow theatre, killing more of their own people than of the Chechen 'terrorists', a clear indication of the fact that we are *all* potentially *Homo sacer*? It is not that some of us are full citizens while others are excluded   an unexpected state of emergency can exclude *every one* of us. This parallel is more revealing than it may appear: in August 2003, it was reported that the Russian government planned to revive one of the most ominous features of Stalinism, the local committees keeping an eye on the population and reporting any 'unusual' activities or persons. Do not some recent US initiatives point in the same direction? Think of 'Operation TIPS' (Terrorist Information and Prevention System), administered by the US Department of Justice and developed in partnership with several other federal agencies, which is one of the five component programmes of the Citizen Corps: a national system for reporting suspicious, and potentially terrorist-related, activity. The programme will involve millions of American workers who, in the course of their daily work, are in a unique position to see potentially unusual or suspicious activity in public places. The Department of Justice is discussing participation with several industry groups whose workers are ideally suited to help in the anti-terrorism effort because their routines allow them to recognize unusual events, and they have expressed a desire for a mechanism for reporting these events to the authorities. This programme offers a way for these workers to report what they see in public areas and along transportation routes. All it will take to volunteer is a telephone or access to the Internet, as tips can be reported on the toll-free hotline or online. Information received will be referred electronically to a point of contact in each State as appropriate. Industries that are interested in participating in this programme will be given printed guidance material, flyers and brochures about the programme, and how to contact the Operation TIPS reporting centre. This information can be distributed to workers or posted in common work areas.

Operation TIPS will be phased in across the country to enable the system to build its capacity to receive an increasing volume of tips. It will be 'a nationwide program giving millions of American truckers, letter carriers, train conductors, ship captains, utility employees, and others a formal way to report suspicious terrorist activity', says the citizencorps.gov website. Involving one million workers in ten cities during the pilot stage, Operation TIPS will be 'a national reporting system. . . . Every participant in this new program will be given an Operation TIPS information sticker to be affixed to the cab of their vehicle or placed in some other public location so that the toll-free number is readily available.' Along the same lines, back in 2002, John Ashcroft unveiled a new and expanded mission for the Neighborhood Watch Program. Hitherto, Neighborhood Watch has been a fairly low-key crime-prevention tool focused on break-ins and burglaries; now, the Bush administration has earmarked it for a broader role, surveillance in the service of the 'war on terror', asking neighbourhood groups to report on people who are 'unfamiliar', or act in ways that are 'suspicious', or 'not normal'.

When we focus on such measures, however, we should completely reject the standard liberal attitude of criticizing them principally as threats to individual freedom, in accordance with the sterile question 'How much freedom should we sacrifice in our defence of freedom against the terrorist threat?' — at this level, we should fully and shamelessly endorse the good old 'totalitarian' Jacobin motto: 'No freedom for the enemies of freedom!' From a radical emancipatory perspective, is 'freedom' actually the highest and most untouchable point of reference? On the contrary, is the notion of freedom not so deeply enmeshed in structurally necessary ambiguities that it should *always* be viewed with elementary suspicion? Think of all the confusion caused by the standard Marxist attempts to oppose a 'merely formal' freedom to 'actual' freedom, against which it was easy for liberals to demonstrate how 'actual freedom' is in effect no freedom at all — how freedom is, in its very essence, formal. Take Étienne Balibar's neologism *égaliberté* ('equaliberty'), which tries to resolve the tired liberal dilemma 'more equality or more freedom?' by means of a truly Freudian symptomal formation-condensation worthy of Heinrich Heine's famous pun 'famillionaire'. Indeed, is not *égaliberté* ultimately a dream equivalent to that of a millionaire treating us in a 'familiar (kind and gentle, human)' way?

Every veteran leftist remembers Marx's reply, in *The Communist Manifesto*, to those who criticized Communists for undermining family, property, and so on: it is the capitalist order itself whose economic dynamic is destroying the traditional family order (incidentally, this is more true today than it was in Marx's time), as well as expropriating the great majority of the population. In the same vein, is it not precisely those who pose today as global defenders of democracy who are actually undermining it? More than a year ago, Jonathan Alter and Alan Derschowitz proposed to 'rethink' human rights so that they could permit torture (of suspected terrorists). In *The Future of Freedom*, Fareed Zakaria, Bush's favoured columnist, already draws a more general conclusion: he locates the threat to freedom in 'overdoing democracy', that is, in the rise of 'illiberal democracy at home and abroad' (the book's subtitle).[21]

This gradual limitation of democracy is clearly perceptible in attempts to 'rethink' the present situation – one is, of course, for democracy and human rights, but one should 'rethink' them, and a series of recent interventions in the public debate give a clear sense of the direction of this 'rethinking'. Let us return to Fareed Zakaria: the immediate lesson of his book for Iraq is clear and unambiguous: yes, the USA should bring democracy to Iraq, but not impose it immediately – there should first be a period of five years or so during which a benevolently authoritarian US-dominated regime would create proper conditions for the effective functioning of democracy.

A paradox of Zakaria's argument is that there is one case which should serve as its perfect example – that of China. Is not the opposition between China and the late USSR precisely the opposition between the authoritarian regime destined to create the conditions for capitalist development and an over-rapid shift to democracy which misfired? So should not Zakaria have supported the notorious crackdown in Tiananmen Square?

As for the USA itself, Zakaria's diagnosis is that 'America is increasingly embracing a simple-minded populism that values popularity and openness as the key measures of legitimacy. . . . The result is a deep imbalance in the American system, more democracy but less liberty.' The remedy is thus to counteract this excessive democratization of democracy' (or 'deMOREcracy') by delegating more power to impartial experts insulated from the democratic fray, such as the independent central banks. Such a diagnosis cannot fail to provoke ironic laughter: today, in the age of alleged 'overdemocratization', the USA and the UK started a war on Iraq against the will of the majority of their own populations, not to mention the international community. And are we not all the time witnessing the imposition of key decisions concerning the global economy (trade agreements, among others) by 'impartial' bodies exempt from democratic control? The idea that, in our post-ideological era, the economy should be depoliticized and run by experts is a common one shared by all participants. Even more fundamentally, is it not ridiculous to complain about 'overdemocratization' at a time when the key economic and geopolitical decisions are, as a rule, not an issue in elections: for at least three decades, what Zakaria is demanding has already been a fact. What we are indeed witnessing today is a split between ideological lifestyle issues, where fierce debates rage and choices are solicited (abortion, gay marriages, and so forth) and basic economic policy, which is presented as a depoliticized domain of expert decisions – the proliferation of 'over-democracy', with its 'excesses' of affirmative action, the 'culture of complaint', and demands for financial and other compensation by victims, is the front whose back is the silent weaving of economic logic.

The obverse of the same tendency to counteract the excesses of 'deMOREcracy' is the open dismissal of any international body that would effectively control the conduct of a war – illustrative here is Kenneth Anderson's 'Who Owns the Rules of War?' whose subtitle makes the point unambiguously clear: 'The war in Iraq demands a rethinking of the international rules of conduct. The outcome could mean less power for neutral, well-meaning human rights groups and more for big-stick-wielding states. That would be a good thing.'[22] The main complaint of this essay is that: 'for the past twenty years, the centre of gravity in estab-lishing, interpreting and shaping the law of war has gradually shifted away from the militaries of leading states and toward more activist human rights organizations'; this tendency is perceived as unbalanced, 'unfair' to the big military powers who intervene in other countries, and biased towards the attacked countries – with the clear conclusion that the military establishments in the 'big-stick-wielding states' should themselves determine the standards by which their actions will be judged. This conclusion is quite consistent with the US rejection of the authority of the Interna-tional Criminal Court over its citizens. In effect – as they would have put it in *The Lord of the Rings*, or a similar neo-Gothic epic – a new Dark Age is descending upon the human race.

What, then, are we blinded to when we dream the dream of the 'war on terror'? Perhaps the first thing to note here is the deep satisfaction of American commentators in ascertaining how, after September 11, the anti-globalist movement lost its *raison d'être* – what if this satisfaction says more than it means to say? What if the war on terror is not so much an answer to the terrorist attacks themselves as an answer to the rise of the anti-globalist movement, a way to contain it and distract attention from it? What if this 'collateral damage' of the war on terror is its true aim? I am tempted to say that we are dealing here with a case of what Stephen Jay Gould would have called (ideological) 'exaptation'. the apparent secondary effect or profit (the fact that the anti-globalist movement is now also listed in the series of 'terrorist' supporters) becomes crucial.

The danger of this 'soft revolution' can be best exemplified by the strange logic of how we accommodate ourselves to catastrophes. In his 'Two Sources of Morality and Religion', Henri Bergson described the strange sensations he experienced on 4 August 1914, when war was declared between France and Germany:

> In spite of my turmoil, and although a war, even a victorious one, appeared to me as a catastrophe, I experienced what [William] James spoke about, a feeling of admiration for the facility of the passage from the abstract to the concrete: who would have thought that such a formidable event can emerge in reality with so little fuss?[23]

The crucial thing here is the modality of the break between before and after: before its outbreak, the war appeared to Bergson '*simultaneously probable and impossible*: a complex and contradictory notion which persisted to the end';[24] afterwards, it suddenly become real *and* possible, and the paradox resides in this retroactive appearance of probability:

> I never pretended that one can insert reality into the past and thus work backwards in time. However, one can without any doubt insert there the possible, or, rather, at every moment, the possible inserts itself there. Insofar as unpredictable and new reality creates itself, its image reflects itself behind itself in the indefinite past: this new reality finds itself all the time having been possible; but it is only at the precise moment of its actual emergence that it *begins to always have been*, and this is why I say that its possibility, which does not precede its reality, will have preceded it once this reality emerges.[25]

The encounter of the Real as impossible is thus always missed: it is experienced either as impossible but not real (the prospect of a forthcoming catastrophe which, however probable we know it is, we do not believe will really happen, and thus dismiss it as impossible) or as real but no longer impossible (once the catastrophe happens, it is 'renormalized', perceived as part of the normal run of things, as always-already having been possible). The gap which makes these paradoxes possible is the one between knowledge and belief: we *know* that the catastrophe is possible, even probable, yet we do not *believe* that it will really happen. And is this not what is happening today, before our very eyes? A decade ago, public debate on torture, or participation by neo-Fascist parties in a West European democratic government, was dismissed as an ethical catastrophe which was impossible, which 'could not really happen'; once it happened, it retroactively grounded its own possibility, and we immediately got accustomed to it.

What, then, is the correct response to the American ideology? Think of the notorious Uncle Sam poster with his finger pointed at the viewer, interpellating him with 'I Want You!' – what if one were to imagine a series of variations (negations, inversions) of it, just as Freud, in 'Drives and their Vicissitudes', provides the genesis of paranoia through multiple variations of the homoerotic statement 'I love him': 'I (do not love him, but) hate him'; '(it is) he (who) loves me', and so on. First, one could simply change the content of the message and imagine, say, a 'benevolent' version of it, like a kind woman addressing the viewer with some pacifist or ecological message ('Mother Earth wants you!'). Then one could imagine a hysterical questioning: what if, instead of 'I want you!', the words from Uncle Sam had been 'Do I really want you? What makes me want you?' Even more subversive here could be the paraphrase of the Priest's famous reply to Joseph K. about the Law from Kafka's *The Trial*: 'Uncle Sam wants nothing from you! He just answers your call when you come to him!' And, to finish the series, what about exactly the same message with just the negation added? 'I *don't* want you!' The difference between these two last versions, which obviously refers to Nietzsche's well-known difference between 'willing nothing' and 'willing nothing(ness) itself': between 'I don't want anything' and 'I *want* nothing', is crucial. The truth resides in the parallax tension between the two versions: Uncle Sam, in effect, addresses me on two levels simultaneously – that is to say, his passive indifference ('I don't want anything from you!') is faked; it conceals an active malevolence and rejection ('I don't want you!'). And the only way to break out of this circle is to return a brutal reply to this last version: 'OK, fuck off then, and stop bothering me!'

The iconography of Saddam Hussein's arrest in December 2003 was, of course, well chosen: endlessly repeated images of his medical examination, with the doctor inspecting his hair (for lice?) and looking into his mouth (no doubt searching for the WMDs hidden there!). Rather than the examination of a home-less, destitute old man, these images recall the Nazis inspecting a Jew in a ghetto raid. While the aim of this operation was clear (to 'desublimate' the figure of Saddam, presenting him as mere miserable scum), we should not forget that it was US propaganda which created what it was now desublimating in the first place: the demonic Saddam as the larger-than-life figure of Evil – it was US propaganda that elevated Saddam, that miserable local thug, into a monstrous sublime figure of Evil. Again, the parallel with the Nazi figure of the Jew is again pertinent here: in both cases, the same figure oscillates between demonic monster and impotent scum. Once he is revealed, the omnipotent scary monster turns into a blotch waiting to be erased.

So should our reaction be that of Cardinal Renato Martino, head of the Pontifical Council for Justice and Peace? He stated that he felt compassion for Saddam, and that the world should have been spared the images of his medical examination after his capture: 'I feel pity at seeing this destroyed man treated like a cow having his teeth checked. I saw this man in his tragedy . . . and I had a sense of compassion.' Martino's intuition was correct: a group of furious and desperate Iraqis would have every right simply to lynch Saddam – but not the USA, for what *they* did.

Now, above all, it is time to remember the great *rapprochement* between Iraq and the USA during the Iraq–Iran war, when Ronald Reagan sent Donald Rumsfeld to Baghdad to work out the details of the US–Iraq collaboration. In 1982, the State Department deleted Iraq from the list of states which support terrorism. In 1986, in the UN Security Council, the USA vetoed the condemnation of Iraq for its use of poisonous gases, against Iranian soldiers. The USA (Dow Chemical) was delivering poisonous gases, unofficially claiming that while their use against civilians was not acceptable, their use against Iranian soldiers was justified, since the survival of Iraq was at stake. No wonder, then, that when, in December 2002, Iraq delivered its 11,800-page report on its WMDs to the Security Council, the report was first filtered by the USA, and thousands of pages disappeared in the version that reached the UN – pages which documented the USA's collaboration with Iraq! This is what Jacques Lacan meant when, in *Seminar XI*, he said: 'I'm certainly looking at the picture. But I myself am in the picture.'[26] I am in the picture in the form of its blind spot, of what is erased from it.

After 9/11, the first codename for the US operation against terrorism was 'Infinite Justice' (later changed in response to American Muslim clerics' objection that only God can exercise infinite justice). Taken seriously, this name is profoundly ambiguous – in philosophical terms, it is 'Kant or Hegel'. Either it means that the Americans have the right ruthlessly to destroy not only all terrorists but also all those who give them material, moral, ideological, etc., support – and this process will be, by definition, endless in the precise sense of Hegelian 'bad infinity': the task will never really be accomplished; there will always be some other terrorist threat (and in fact, in April 2002, Dick Cheney frankly admitted that the 'war on terror' will probably never end, at least not in our lifetimes). Or it means that the justice exercised must be truly infinite in the strict Hegelian sense: that, in relating to others, it has to relate to itself – in short, that it has to ask how we ourselves, who exercise justice, are involved in what we are fighting against. When, on 22 September 2001, Jacques Derrida received the Theodor Adorno Award, he referred in his acceptance speech to the WTC attacks: 'My unconditional compassion, addressed to the victims of September 11, does not prevent me from saying this out loud: with regard to this crime, I do not believe that anyone is politically guiltless.' This self-relating, this inclusion of oneself in the picture, is the only true 'infinite justice'.

The real question about justice is thus: now, after Saddam is put on trial, who will judge the warriors on terror?

Appendix I: *Canis a non Canendo*

The Liberal Fake

Recall the well-known (true) story, retold again and again, of how, a century ago, a ruling by the US Supreme Court defined as 'Negro' anyone with even a minimum of African-American blood – 1/64th of your ancestry was enough, even if you looked totally white. What is wrong with the passionate retelling of such stories, which is usually accompanied by exclamations like 'You see, this was even worse than the Nazis, for whom you counted as Jewish only if a quarter or more of your ancestry was Jewish!'? The very focus on the excess automatically makes acceptable a more 'moderate' form of the racist exclusion – say, 'only' a quarter or a third of African-American blood. . . .

This story perfectly encapsulates the true problem with politicians such as Le Pen in France. A close look at how Le Pen made it into the second round of the French presidential elections in 2002 reveals the true stakes of the widespread emotion of 'fear' and 'shame', even panic, that Le Pen's first-round success generated among many a democratic leftist. The cause of this panic was not Le Pen's percentage as such, but the fact that he finished *second* among the candidates, instead of Lionel Jospin, the 'logical' candidate for this place. The panic was triggered by the fact that, in the democratic Imaginary of multiparty states in which the political field is bi-polar, with two big parties or blocs exchanging power, second place symbolically indicates the *eligibility* of a candidate: 'Le Pen finished second' entails that he is considered eligible, a viable candidate for power. This is what disturbed the silent pact of today's liberal democracies that allow political freedom to everyone . . . on condition that a set of implicit rules clearly limits the scope of those who can actually be elected.

So, then, was the thing that made Le Pen unfit for election simply the fact that he is heterogeneous to the liberal-democratic order, a foreign body in it? There is more to it: the misfortune (and role) of Le Pen was to introduce certain topics (the foreign threat, the necessity to limit immigration, and so forth) which were then silently taken over not only by the conservative parties, but even by the *de facto* policies of 'Socialist' governments. I am almost tempted to say that, had there been no Le Pen in France, he would have had to be invented: he is the perfect figure whom one loves to hate, the hatred for whom guarantees the general liberal-democratic 'pact', the pathetic identification with the democratic values of tolerance and respect for diversity – however, after shouting, 'Horrible! How dark and uncivilized! Wholly unacceptable! A threat to our basic democratic values!', the outraged liberals proceed to act like 'Le Pen with a human face', to do the same thing in a more 'civilized' way, along the lines of 'But the racist populists are manipulating the legitimate concerns of ordinary people, so we do have to take some measures!' . . . Today, the alleged need to 'regulate' the status of immigrants, and so on, is part of the mainstream consensus: as the leading French Socialist Laurent Fabius put it, Le Pen did ask the right questions, it is just that he provided the wrong answers. The 'shame' apropos of Le Pen was thus the shame that arises when the hypocritical masks are torn off, and we are directly confronted with our true stance.

We have here a kind of perverted Hegelian 'negation of

negation': in a first negation, the populist Right disturbs the aseptic liberal consensus by giving voice to passionate dissent, clearly arguing against the 'foreign threat'; in a second negation, the 'decent' democratic Centre, in the very gesture of pathetically rejecting this populist Right, integrates its message in a 'civilized' way – in between, the *entire field* of background 'unwritten rules' has already changed so much that no one even notices, and everyone is simply relieved that the anti-democratic threat is over. And the true danger is that something similar will happen with the 'war on terror': 'extremists' such as John Ashcroft will be discredited, but their legacy will remain, imperceptibly woven into the invisible ethical fabric of our societies. Their defeat will be their ultimate triumph: they will no longer be needed, since their message will be incorporated into the mainstream. This defeat will simultaneously signal the defeat of democracy itself, its gradual change into a travesty of itself, its impotence in the face of a right-wing populist threat.

Phenomena such as these give us a clear indication of what the Left has been doing in the last few decades: ruthlessly pursuing the path of *giving way*, of accommodating itself, of making the 'necessary compromises' with the declared enemy (just as the Church had to compromise on the essentials in order to redefine its role in modern secular society) by reconciling opposites, that is, reconciling its own position with that of the declared opponent: it stands for socialism, but can fully endorse economic Thatcherism; it stands for science, but can fully endorse the rule of the multitude of opinions; it stands for true popular democracy, but can also play the game of politics as spectacle and electoral spin; it stands for principled fidelity, but can be totally pragmatic; it stands for the freedom of the press, but can flatter and get the support of Murdoch. . . . In the early days of his government, Tony Blair liked to paraphrase the famous joke from Monty Python's *Life of Brian* ('All right, but apart from sanitation, medicine, education, wine, public order, irrigation, roads, the fresh-water system and public health, what have the Romans ever done for us?') in order ironically to disarm his critics: 'They betrayed socialism. True, they brought more social security, they did a lot for healthcare and education, and so on, but, in spite of all that, they betrayed socialism.' As it is clear today, it is, rather, the reverse which applies: 'We remain socialists. True, we practise Thatcherism in economics, we attack asylum-seekers, beggars and single mothers, we made a deal with Murdoch, and so on, but, none the less, we're still socialists.'

As I have already pointed out, during the 'golden age' of the twentieth century, great conservatives often accomplished the tough jobs for the liberals. Today, the opposite scenario is more the rule: the new Third-Way Left does the job for economic conservative liberals, dismantling the welfare state, pushing privatization to its logical conclusion, and so on.

In his brilliant analysis of the political *imbroglio* of the French revolution of 1848, Marx pointed out the paradoxical status of the ruling Party of Order. It was a coalition of the two royalist wings (Bourbons and Orleanists). However, since the two parties were, by definition, unable to find a common denominator at the level of royalism (one could not be a royalist in general, since one had to support a certain determinate royal house), the only way for the two to unite was under the banner of the 'anonymous kingdom of the Republic': the only way to be a royalist in general was to be a republican.[1] And, *mutatis mutandis*, is not something similar going on today? As we all know, capital nowadays is split into two fractions (traditional industrial capital and 'postmodern' digital-informational capital), and the only way for the two fractions to find a common denominator is under the banner of the 'anonymous capitalism of social democracy': today, the only way to be a capitalist *in general* is to be a (Third Way) social democrat. This is how the Left–Right opposition works now: it is the new Third Way Left which stands for the interests of capital as such, in its totality (that is, in relative independence from its particular fractions); while today's Right, as a rule, advocates the interests of some particular layer of capital in opposition to other sectors – which is why, paradoxically, in order to win a majority, it has to augment its electoral base by directly appealing to select parts of the working class as well. No wonder, then, that it is mostly in the modern right-wing parties that we find explicit references to the interests of the working class (protectionist measures against cheap foreign labour and cheap imports, and the like).

The stance of simply condemning the postmodern Left for its accommodation, however, is also false, since one should ask the obvious difficult question: *what, in fact, was the alternative?* If today's 'post-politics' is opportunistic pragmatism with no principles, then the predominant leftist reaction to it can be aptly characterized as 'principled opportunism': one simply sticks to old formulae (defence of the welfare state, and so on) and calls them 'principles', dispensing with the detailed analysis of how the situation has changed – and thus retaining one's position of Beautiful Soul. The inherent stupidity of the 'principled' Left is clearly discernible in its standard criticism of any analysis which proposes a more complex picture of the situation, renouncing any simple prescriptions on how to act: 'there is no clear political stance involved in your theory' – and this from people with no stance but their 'principled opportunism'. Against such a stance, one should have the courage to affirm that, in a situation like today's, the only way really to remain open to a revolutionary opportunity is to renounce facile calls to direct action, which necessarily involve us in an activity where things change so that the totality remains the same. Today's predicament is that, if we succumb to the urge of directly 'doing something' (engaging in the anti-globalist struggle, helping the poor . . .), we will certainly and undoubtedly contribute to the reproduction of the existing order. The only way to lay the foundations for a true, radical change is to withdraw from the compulsion to act, to 'do nothing' – thus opening up the space for a different kind of activity.

Today's anti-globalization movement seems to be caught in the antinomy of de- and reterritorialization: on the one hand, there are those who want to reterritorialize capitalism (conservatives, ecologists, partisans of the nation-state and champions of local roots or traditions); on the other, there are those who want an even more radical deterritorialization, liberated from the constraints of capital. But is this opposition not too simple? Is it not ultimately a false alternative? Is not the capitalist 'territory' (everything must pass through the grid of market exchange) the very form and vector of radical deterritorialization – its operator, as it were? (And does the same not go for the nation-state, this operator of the erasure of local traditions?) Positivity and negativity are inextricably intertwined here, which is why the true aim should be a new balance, a new *form* of de- and reterritorialization. This brings us back to the central sociopolitical antinomy of late capitalism: the way its pluralist dynamic of permanent deterritorialization coexists with its opposite, the paranoid logic of the One, thereby confirming that, perhaps, in the Deleuzian opposition between schizophrenia and paranoia, between the multitude and the One, we are dealing with two sides of the same coin.

Were the Left to choose the 'principled' attitude of fidelity to its old programme, it would simply marginalize itself. The task is a much harder one: thoroughly to rethink the leftist project, beyond the alternative of 'accommodation to new circumstances' and sticking with the old slogans. Apropos of the disintegration of 'state socialism' two decades ago, we should not forget that, at approximately the same time, Western social-democratic welfarist ideology was also dealt a crucial blow, that it also ceased to function as the Imaginary able to arouse a collective passionate following. The notion that 'the time of the welfare state has past' is a piece of commonly accepted wisdom today. What these two defeated ideologies shared was the notion that humanity as a collective subject has the capacity somehow to limit impersonal and anonymous sociohistoric development, to steer it in a desired direction. Today, such a notion is quickly dismissed as 'ideological' and/or 'totalitarian': the social process is perceived as dominated by an anonymous Fate which eludes social control. The rise of global capitalism is presented to us as such a Fate, against which we cannot fight – either we adapt to it or we fall out of step with history, and are crushed. The only thing we can do is to make global capitalism as human as possible, to fight for 'global capitalism with a human face' (this, ultimately, is what the Third Way is – or, rather, *was* – about).

Act, Evil, and Antigone

Whenever a political project takes a radical turn, up pops the inevitable blackmail: 'Of course these goals are desirable in themselves; if we do all this, however, international capital will boycott us, the growth rate will fall, and so on.' The sound barrier – the qualitative leap that occurs when one expands the quantity of resistance from local communities to wider social circles (up to the state itself) – will have to be broken, and the risk will have to be taken to organize larger and larger social circles along the lines of the self-organization of excluded marginal communities. Many fetishes will have to be broken here: who cares if growth stalls, or even becomes negative? Have we not had enough of the high growth rate whose effects on the social organism were felt mostly in the guise of new forms of poverty and dispossession? What about a negative growth that would translate into a qualitatively better, not higher, standard of living for the wider popular strata? *That* would be a political *act* today – to break the spell of automatically endorsing the existing political framework, to break out of the debilitating alternative 'either we just directly endorse free-market globalization, or we make impossible promises along the lines of magic formulae about how to have one's cake and eat it, about how to combine globalization with social solidarity'.

Nowhere is today's resistance to the political act proper more palpable than in the obsession with 'radical Evil', the negative of the act. It is as if the supreme Good today is that nothing should really happen, which is why the only way we can imagine an act is in the guise of a catastrophic disturbance, a traumatic explosion of Evil. Susan Neiman was right to emphasize why September 11 took so many leftist social critics by surprise: Fascism was, for them, the last appearance of a directly transparent Evil.[2] Since 1945 they have been, for decades, perfecting the art of 'symptomal' reading, a mode of reading which taught us to recognize Evil in the guise of its opposite: liberal democracy itself legitimizes social orders which generate genocide and slaughter; today, massive crimes result from anonymous bureaucratic logic (what Chomsky called the invisible 'backroom boys'). With September 11, however, they suddenly encountered an Evil which fits the most naive Hollywood image: a secret organization of fanatics who fully intend, and plan in detail, a terrorist attack whose aim is to kill thousands of random civilian victims. It is as if Arendt's 'banality of evil' was again inverted: if anything, the al-Qaeda suicide attackers were not in any sense 'banal', but effectively 'demonic'. So, it seemed to leftist intellectuals that were they directly to condemn these attacks, they would somehow undo the results of their complex analyses, and regress to the Hollywood-fundamentalist level of George W. Bush.

In a further elaboration, I would like to propose four modes of political Evil which, yet again, form a kind of Greimasian semiotic square: totalitarian 'idealist' Evil, accomplished with the best intentions (revolutionary terror); authoritarian Evil, whose aim is simple corruption and power (not any higher goal); 'terrorist' fundamentalist Evil, bent on the ruthless infliction of massive damage, destined to cause fear and panic; and Arendtian 'banal'

Evil, accomplished by anonymous bureaucratic structures. The first thing to note here, however, is that the Marquis de Sade, the epitome of modern Evil, fits none of these four modes: he is so attractive today because, in his works, the evil characters are larger-than-life demonic personalities who also reflect on what they are doing, and act in a fully intentional manner – the very opposite of Arendt's 'banality of Evil', an Evil totally incommensurate with the grey, average, petty-bourgeois 'desk-killer' characters à la Eichmann. It is here that Pasolini, in his *120 Days of Sodom*, is wrong: as Neiman puts it, 'Sade and Auschwitz have little in common. It is unlikely that a general formula will be found to unite them, and any attempt to do so may obscure what is morally important in each.'[3]

Thus 'Evil' is a much more complex category than it may appear. It is not a simple eccentric obscenity to compare Angelis Silesius' famous mystical statement 'The rose is without a "why" ' with Primo Levi's experience in Auschwitz. When Levi, thirsty, tried to reach for a piece of snow on the windowsill of his barracks, the guard outside yelled at him to move back; in reply to Levi's perplexed 'Why?' – why the refusal of such an act, which hurt no one and broke no rules – the guard replied: 'There is no "why" here in Auschwitz.' Perhaps the coincidence of these two 'whys' is the ultimate 'infinite judgement' of the twentieth century: the groundless fact of a rose enjoying its own existence meets its 'oppositional determination' in the groundless prohibition springing from the pure *jouissance* of the guard – just for the sake of it. In other words, what, in the domain of nature, is pure, pre-ethical innocence returns (quite literally) with a vengeance in the domain of nature in the guise of the pure caprice of Evil.

The cause of today's persistence of the topic of Evil was succinctly captured by Habermas: 'Secular languages which only eliminate the substance once intended leave irritations. When sin was converted to culpability, and the breaking of divine commands to an offence against human laws, something was lost.'[4] This is why the secular-humanist reaction to phenomena such as the Holocaust or the Gulag (and others) is experienced as insufficient: in order to attain the same level as such phenomena, something much stronger is needed, something akin to the old religious trope of a cosmic perversion or catastrophe in which the world itself is 'out of joint'. Therein lies the paradox of the theological significance of the Holocaust: although it is usually conceived of as the ultimate challenge to theology (if there is a God, and if He is good, how could He have allowed such a horror to take place?), it is at the same time only theology that can provide the framework which enables us somehow to approach the scope of this catastrophe. God's failure to help us, and prevent catastrophes like the Holocaust, is not the whole story: the catastrophe was so gigantic that the blame for it cannot be put simply on us humans – it is as if we still need some kind of divine dimension to blame.

It is this background that enables us to deploy the paradigmatic figure of today's Evil, best exemplified by the ambiguity of the dénouement in Bryan Singer's neo-noir film *The Usual Suspects*: at the very (final) moment, when we are led to identify the crippled weakling Verbal Klint as Keyser Soeze, the invisible, all-powerful master criminal, and are thus finally able to tie the threads of the narrative together, this very narrative is denounced as a fake, an impromptu, improvised lie based on fragments perceptible in the very room where the interrogation of Klint took place ('Kobayashi', the name of Soeze's mysterious Oriental agent, is revealed to be the name printed on the bottom of the mug that the police interrogator was drinking out of, and so forth). That is the ultimate ambiguity: does Keyser Soeze, this invisible, all-powerful agent of Evil, exist at all, or is he the phantasmatic invention of the pitiful Klint? Or, in a more complex way, is Soeze the fabricator of his own myth? In a properly dialectical way, the very 'quilting point [*point de capiton*]' which promises to establish the true narrative, resolving all inconsistencies, radically undermines our narrative security, throwing us into an abyssal echo chamber of deception.[5]

We all know the cliché about conspiracy theories being the poor man's ideology: when individuals lack the elementary cognitive mapping capabilities and resources that would enable them to locate their place within a social totality, they invent conspiracy theories which provide an ersatz mapping, explaining all the complexities of social life as the result of a hidden conspiracy. However, as Fredric Jameson likes to point out, this ideologico-critical dismissal is not enough: in today's global capitalism, we *are* all too often dealing with real 'conspiracies'. For example, the destruction of the Los Angeles public transport network in the 1950s was not an expression of some 'objective logic of capital', but the result of an explicit 'conspiracy' between car companies, road construction companies and public agencies – and the same goes for many 'tendencies' in contemporary urban development. The dismissal of the 'paranoid' ideological dimension of conspiracy theories (the supposition of a mysterious all-powerful Master, and so on) should alert us to *actual* 'conspiracies' going on all the time. Today, the ultimate ideology would be the self-complacent critico-ideological dismissal of all conspiracies as mere fantasies. So, back to *The Usual Suspects*: the worst ideological reading of the film would have been to read it as the assertion of the ideology of universalized textuality ('there is no reality, just a multitude of contingent stories we are telling ourselves about ourselves').

The concept of radical, 'irrepresentable' Evil, be it the Holocaust or the Gulag, is therefore the constitutive limit and point of reference of today's predominant notion of democracy: 'democracy' means avoiding the 'totalitarian' extreme; it is defined as a permanent struggle against the 'totalitarian' temptation to close the gap, to (pretend to) act on behalf of the Thing itself. Ironically, it is thus as if one should turn around the well-known Augustinian notion of Evil as having no positive substance or force of its own, being just the absence of Good: Good itself is the absence of Evil, the distance towards the Evil Thing.

It is this liberal blackmail of dismissing every radical political act as evil that one should thoroughly reject – even when it is painted in Lacanian colours, as is the case in Yannis Stavrakakis's recent critical reply to my reading of *Antigone*, which focuses on the danger of what he calls the 'absolutization' of the event, which then leads to a totalitarian *désastre*. When Stavrakakis writes that 'fidelity to an event can flourish and avoid absolutization only as an infidel fidelity, only within the framework of another fidelity, fidelity to the openness of the political space and to the awareness of the constitutive impossibility of a final suture of the social', [6] he thereby surreptitiously introduces a difference, which can be given various names, between the unconditional-ethical and the pragmatico-political: the original fact is the lack, the opening, which pertains to human finitude, and all positive acts always fall short of this primordial lack; thus we have what Derrida calls the unconditional ethical injunction, impossible to fulfil, and positive acts, interventions, which remain strategic interventions. . . . One should put forward two arguments against this position:

1. 'Acts' in Lacan's sense precisely suspend this gap between the impossible injunction and the positive intervention – they are 'impossible' not in the sense of 'it is impossible that they might happen', but in the sense of the impossible that *did happen*. *This* is why Antigone was of interest to me: her act is not a strategic intervention which maintains the gap towards the impossible Void; rather, it tends to enact the impossible 'absolutely'. I am well aware of the 'lure' of such an act – but I claim that, in Lacan's later versions of the act, this moment of 'madness' beyond strategic intervention remains. In this precise sense, the notion of the act not only does not contradict the 'lack in the Other' which, according to Stavrakakis, I overlook – it directly presupposes it: it is only through an act that I effectively assume the big Other's nonexistence, that is, I enact the impossible: namely, what appears as impossible within the co-ordinates of the existing socio-symbolic order.

2. There *are* (also) political acts, for politics cannot be reduced to the level of strategic-pragmatic interventions. In a radical political act, the opposition between 'crazy' destructive gesture and a strategic political decision momentarily breaks down – which is why it is theoretically and politically wrong to oppose strategic political acts, risky as they may be, to radical 'suicidal' gestures *à la* Antigone: gestures of pure self-destructive

ethical insistence with, apparently, no political goal. The point is not simply that, once we are thoroughly engaged in a political project, we are ready to put everything at stake for it, including our lives; but, more precisely, that *only such an 'impossible' gesture of pure expenditure can change the very co-ordinates of what is strategically possible within a historical constellation.* This is the key point: an act is neither a strategic intervention *in* the existing order, nor its 'crazy' destructive *negation*; an act is an 'excessive', trans-strategic intervention which redefines the rules and contours of the existing order.

So what about the criticism that Antigone does not only risk death or suspend the symbolic order – my criteria for a political act but actively strives for death, for symbolic and real death, thereby displaying a purity of desire beyond any sociopolitical transformative action? First, is Antigone's act really outside politics, 'apolitical'? Is not her defiance of the order of supreme power (Creon, who acts on behalf of the common good) political, albeit in a negative way? In certain extreme circumstances, is not such 'apolitical' defiance on behalf of 'decency' or 'old customs' even the very model of heroic political resistance? Second, her gesture is not simply a pure desire for death – had it been so, she could have directly killed herself and spared the people around her all the fuss. Hers was not a pure symbolic striving for death, but an unconditional insistence on a particular symbolic ritual.

Risking the Step Outside

This brings us to the key dilemma: what the reference to democracy involves is the rejection of radical attempts to 'step outside', to risk a radical break, to pursue the trend of self-organized collectives in zones outside the law. Arguably, the greatest literary monument to such a utopia comes from an unexpected source: Mario Vargas Llosa's *The War of the End of the World* (1981), a novel about Canudos, an outlaw community deep in the Brazilian heartland which was home to prostitutes, freaks, beggars, bandits and the most wretched of the poor. Canudos, led by an apocalyptic prophet, was a utopian space without money, property, taxes and marriage. In 1897, it was destroyed by the military forces of the Brazilian government. The echoes of Canudos are clearly discernible in today's *favelas* in Latin American megalopolises: are they not, in some sense, the first 'liberated territories', the cells of future self-organized societies? Are not institutions such as community kitchens models of 'socialized' communal local life? The liberated territory of Canudos in Bahia will remain for ever the model of a space of emancipation, of an alternative community which completely negates the existing space of the state. Everything is to be endorsed here, up to and including religious 'fanaticism'. It is as if, in such communities, *the Benjaminian other side of historical Progress, that of the vanquished, acquires a space of its own*. Utopia *existed* here for a brief period of time – this is the only way to account for the 'irrational', excessive, violence of the destruction of these communities (in the Brazil of 1897, *all* the inhabitants of Canudos, children and women included, were slaughtered, as if the very memory of the possibility of freedom had to be erased – and this by a government which presented itself as 'progressive' liberal-democratic-republican . . .). Throughout history, such communities have exploded from time to time as passing phenomena, as sites of eternity that interrupted the flow of temporal progress – one should have the courage to recognize them in the wide span from the Jesuit *reduciones* in eighteenth-century Paraguay (brutally destroyed by the joint action of Spanish and Portuguese armies) to the settlements controlled by Sendero Luminoso in Peru in the 1990s.

There is a will to accomplish the 'leap of faith' and *step outside* the global circuit at work here, a will which was expressed in an extreme and terrifying manner in a well-known incident from the Vietnam War: after the US Army occupied a local village, their doctors vaccinated the children on the left arm in order to demonstrate their humanitarian care; when, the day after, the village was retaken by the Vietcong, they cut off the left arms of all the vaccinated children. . . . Although it is difficult to sustain as a literal model to follow, this complete rejection of the enemy precisely in its caring 'humanitarian' aspect, no matter what the cost, has to be endorsed in its basic intention. In a similar way, when Sendero Luminoso took over a village, they did not focus on killing the soldiers or policemen stationed there, but more on the UN or US agricultural consultants or health workers trying to help the local peasants – after lecturing them for hours, and then forcing them to confess their complicity with imperialism publicly, they shot them. Brutal as this procedure was, it was rooted in an acute insight: they, not the police or the army, were the true danger, the enemy at its most perfidious, since they were 'lying in the guise of truth' – the more they were 'innocent' (they 'really' tried to help the peasants), the more they served as a tool of the USA. It is only such a blow against the enemy at his best, at the point where the enemy 'indeed helps us', that displays true revolutionary autonomy and 'sovereignty' (to use this term in its Bataillean sense). If one adopts the attitude of 'let us take from the enemy what is good, and reject or even fight against what is bad', one is already caught in the liberal trap of 'humanitarian aid'.

Since, today, capitalism defines and structures the totality of human civilization, every 'Communist' territory was and is – again, despite its horrors and failures – a kind of 'liberated territory', as Fredric Jameson put it apropos of Cuba. What we are dealing with here is the old structural notion of the gap between the Space and the positive content that fills it: although, in terms of their positive content, the Communist regimes were mostly a dismal failure, generating terror and misery, at the same time they opened up a certain space, the space of utopian expectations which, among other things, enabled us to measure the failure of really existing socialism itself. (What the anti-Communist dissidents tend to overlook as a rule is that the very space from which they themselves criticized and denounced the everyday terror and misery was opened up and sustained by the Communist breakthrough, by its attempt to escape the logic of Capital.) This is how one should understand Alain Badiou's *'mieux vaut un désastre qu'un désêtre* [better a disaster than a lack of being]', so shocking to the liberal sensibility: better the worst Stalinist terror than the most liberal capitalist democracy. Of course, the moment one compares the positive content of the two, welfare-state capitalist democracy is incomparably better – what redeems Stalinist 'totalitarianism' is the formal aspect, the *space* it opens up. Can we imagine a utopian point at which this subterranean level of the utopian Other Space would unite with the positive space of 'normal' social life? The key political question here is: is there, in our 'postmodern' time, still a space for such communities? Are they limited to the undeveloped outskirts (*favelas*, ghettos), or is a space for them emerging in the very heart of the 'post-industrial' landscape? Can one make a wild wager that the dynamics of 'postmodern' capitalism, with its rise of new eccentric geek communities, provides a new opportunity here? That, perhaps for the first time in history, the logic of alternative communities can be grafted on to the latest stage of technology?

The main form of such alternative communities in the twentieth century were so-called workers' councils ('soviets') – (almost) everybody in the West loved them, including liberals such as Hannah Arendt, who perceived in them an echo of the Ancient Greek life of the *polis*. Throughout the epoch of Really Existing Socialism (RES), the secret hope of 'democratic socialists' was the direct democracy of the 'soviets', local councils as the form of the self-organization of the people; and it is deeply symptomatic how, with the decline of RES, this emancipatory shadow which haunted it all the time has also disappeared – is this not the ultimate confirmation of the fact that the conciliar version of 'democratic socialism' was just a spectral double of the 'bureaucratic' RES, its inherent transgression with no substantial positive content of its own, that is, unable to serve as the permanent basic organizational principle of a society? What both RES and conciliar democracy shared was a belief in the possibility of a self-transparent organization of society which would preclude political 'alienation' (state apparatuses, institutionalized rules of political life, legal order, police, and so forth), and is not the basic experience of the end of RES precisely the rejection of this *shared* feature, the resigned 'postmodern' acceptance of the fact that society is a complex network of 'subsystems', which is why a certain level of 'alienation' is constitutive of social life, so that a totally self-transparent society is a utopia with totalitarian potential?[7] (In this sense, it is Habermas who is 'postmodern', in contrast to Adorno who, despite all his political compromises, remained to the end attached to a radically utopian vision of revolutionary redemption.)

However, are things really that simple? First, direct democracy is not only still alive in many places, such as the *favelas*, it is even being 'reinvented' and given a new boost by the rise the 'post-industrial' digital culture (do not the descriptions of the new 'tribal' communities of computer-hackers often evoke the logic of conciliar democracy?). Secondly, the awareness that politics is a complex game in which a certain level of institutional alienation is irreducible should not lead us to ignore the fact that there is still a line of separation which divides those who are 'in' from those who are 'out', excluded from the space of the *polis* – there are citizens, and then there is the spectre of the excluded *Homo sacer* haunting them all. In other words, even 'complex' contemporary societies still rely on the basic divide between included and excluded. The fashionable notion of the 'multitude' is insufficient precisely in so far as it cuts across this divide: there is a multitude *within* the system and a multitude of those *excluded*, and simply to encompass them both within the scope of the same notion amounts to the same obscenity as equating starvation with dieting. The excluded do not simply dwell in a psychotic non-structured Outside: they have (and are forced into) their own self-organization (or, rather, they are forced into organizing themselves) – and one of the names (and practices) of this self-organization was precisely 'conciliar democracy'.

But should we still call it 'democracy'? At this point, it is crucial to avoid what one cannot but call the 'democratic trap'. Many 'radical' leftists accept the legalistic logic of the 'transcendental guarantee': they refer to 'democracy' as the ultimate guarantee of those who are aware that there is no guarantee. That is to say: since no political act can claim a direct foundation in some transcendent figure of the big Other (of the 'we are just instruments of a higher Necessity or Will' type), since every such act involves the risk of a contingent decision, nobody has the right to impose his or her choice on others – which means that every collective choice has to be democratically legitimized. From this perspective, democracy is not so much the guarantee of the right choice as a kind of opportunistic insurance against possible failure: if things turn out badly, I can always say that we are all responsible. . . . Consequently, this last refuge must be dropped; one should fully assume the risk. The only adequate position is the one advocated by Lukács in *History and Class Consciousness*: democratic struggle should not be fetishized; it is one of the forms of struggle, and its choice should be determined by a global strategic assessment of circumstances, not by its ostensibly superior intrinsic value. Like the Lacanian analyst, a political agent has to engage in acts which can be authorized only by themselves, for which there is no external guarantee.

An authentic political act can be, in terms of its form, a democratic one as well as a non-democratic one. There are some elections or referenda in which 'the impossible happens' – remember the referendum on divorce decades ago in Italy: to the great surprise even of the Left, which distrusted the people, the pro-divorce side won convincingly, so that the Left, privately sceptical, was ashamed of its distrust. (There were elements of the act even in Mitterrand's unexpected first electoral victory.) It is only in *such* cases that one is justified in saying that, over and above the mere numerical majority, the people have effectively spoken in a substantial sense of the term. On the other hand, an authentic act of popular will can also occur in the form of a violent revolution, or a progressive military dictatorship, and so on. In this precise sense, Khrushchev's 1956 speech denouncing Stalin's crimes was a true political act – as William Taubman put it, after this speech: 'the Soviet regime never fully recovered, and neither did he'.[8] Although the opportunistic motives for this daring move are plain enough, there was clearly more than mere calculation to it, a kind of reckless excess which cannot be accounted for by strategic reasoning. After this speech, things were never the same again, the fundamental dogma of infallible leadership was undermined; so it was no wonder that, as a reaction to the speech, the entire *nomenklatura* sank into temporary paralysis.

Too Radical for Democracy?

It is here that one should apply Ernesto Laclau's and Chantal Mouffe's opposition of difference and antagonism, but turn it against Laclau himself. The respective theoretical fields of Laclau/Mouffe and Negri/Hardt are clearly opposed along the lines of Kant versus Spinoza: the irreducible Absence, gap, failure to reach self-identity, versus the positivity of pure immanence. True universality can be best captured through Laclau's opposition of antagonism and difference: when we are dealing with a system of differences (a structured social body), its 'universality' is not the encompassing totality which includes all parts, or some feature shared by all of them, but its 'antagonism' as a certain difference which cuts diagonally across all parts of the system of difference (the social body). This is what Badiou attributes to Saint Paul, as his great invention: the invention of a 'militant universalism'. The position of universality is not simply one which floats above differences, mediating or encompassing them all, but the position of knowing how to traverse the field with an additional, more radical difference, a difference which cuts each particular part from within. This is how the 'universality' of Christianity functions in Saint Paul's work: when he wrote, 'there are no Jews or Greeks, no men or women', this suspension of differences is not achieved through an all-encompassing shared universal feature ('they are all human') – if we conceive of it in this way, it is easy to criticize Saint Paul for qualifying this inclusion, limiting it to those who accept Christ as their saviour, while those who do not accept Christ are excluded. On the contrary, Saint Paul's point is precisely that these oppositions do not matter, what matters is the *struggle* between Life and Death, between Salvation and Loss. How, then, does this relate to democracy? Let us start with Laclau and Mouffe's basic insight into how democracy relies on the translation of antagonism into agonism:

A pluralistic democratic order supposes that the opponent is not seen as an enemy to be destroyed, but as an adversary whose existence is legitimate and must be tolerated. We will fight against his/her ideas, but we will not put into question his/her right to defend them. This category of the adversary does not eliminate the antagonism, though. And it should be distinguished from the liberal notion of the competitor, with which it is sometimes identified. An adversary is a legitimate enemy, an enemy with whom we have in common a shared adhesion to the ethico-political principles of democracy. But our disagreement concerning their meaning and implementation is not one that can be resolved through rational agreement, hence the antagonistic element in the relation. To come to accept the position of the adversary is to undergo a radical change in political identity. To be sure, compromises are possible; they are part of the process of politics. But they should be seen as temporary respites in an ongoing confrontation.[9]

The problem here is that this translation of antagonism into agonism, into the regulated game of political competition, by definition involves a constitutive exclusion, and it is this exclusion that Laclau fails to thematize. His analysis is too compressed in so far as it uses difference and antagonism as extreme notions equally applicable to all sociopolitical phenomena: as Laclau repeats again and again, every political agent is located between the two extremes – in other words, that there can be neither a pure antagonism (that would entail the erasure of all differences, the total homogenization of the entire social field into two opposed forces, the end of all complex 'overdetermination' and struggle for hegemony, as in the vulgar Marxist dream of the final moment of 'pure' class struggle in which all masks fall and there are just

Us against Them) nor a pure difference (which would entail a totally symbolized hierarchical social body in which every agent would be fully identified by a structural place within the social totality, so that, again, the struggle for hegemony would be over). What this way of conceptualizing the situation obfuscates, however, is the fact that, within every society, antagonism is operative also as the principle of *excluding* a series of agents from the 'legitimate' social body – in other words, that the self-organization of the excluded is radically different from that of those whose identity is admitted into the 'legitimate' social body.

And, to avoid a tedious misunderstanding, this does not entail the claim that those who are excluded are 'totally outside' if one examines the situation more closely, one can, of course, immediately establish how the two levels interpenetrate and echo each other – how, for example, the space of the excluded often reproduces the most brutal authoritarian features of the state; or, on the other side, how the legitimate state is often sustained by 'excluded' (publicly disavowed) practices. These echoes and interpenetrations, however, concern the positive content which fills in the two different structural places. To return to the example of the Canudos community: of course, many of its features were borrowed from the premodern regime (they defined themselves as royalists, as protectors of the public role of the Church against the republican drive for modernization of the Brazilian state), but what really mattered was that all these elements were transfigured (even transubstantiated) by the space in which they (re)appeared. It is thus trivial and unproductive to point out how the gap between mainstream Brazilian society and the Canudos alternative community was not total, how there were elements of difference and antagonism in both of them; what matters is that, in passing from mainstream society to Canudos, we accomplish a key 'jump from quantity to quality', from antagonism subordinated to differences to the predominant role of antagonism.

For this reason, it seems politically much more fertile and theoretically much more adequate to limit 'democracy' to the translation of antagonism into agonism: while democracy acknowledges the irreducible plurality of interests, ideologies, narratives, and so on, it excludes those who, as we put it, reject the democratic rules of the game – liberal democrats are quite right in claiming that populism is inherently 'anti-democratic'.[10] This brings us to the so-called 'normative deficit' of Laclau's theory of hegemony:

> Many times I have been asked if there is not a normative deficit in the theory of hegemony that I have elaborated with Chantal Mouffe in *Hegemony and Socialist Strategy* – the argument being that the theorization of hegemony is an objective neutral description of what is going on in the world, while the book also makes a normative choice (radical democracy) which does not necessarily follow from such theorization. My answer is twofold. Firstly that, as I have argued earlier on, there is no such thing as a neutral factual description: the system of supposedly descriptive categories that we have used corresponds to 'facts' which are only such for somebody who is living within the socialist tradition and has experienced the set of defeats, social transformation and renaissance of hopes to which we make allusion. Secondly,

that within that normative/descriptive complex it makes perfect sense to advocate the normative displacement involved in the notion of 'radical democracy'. The latter is the result of a pluralization of social struggles anchored in the new structures of contemporary capitalism.[11]

This answer is clearly insufficient on account of its purely formal character: Laclau's answer to the criticism (which, incidentally, I also made) regarding how he closes the gap between his theory of hegemony and his political choice of 'radical democracy' is that we do not live in an abstract world, but are finite engaged agents thrown into a concrete universe of sedimented practices, so that even our most neutral disinterested descriptions are already marked by certain normative presuppositions that pertain to the universe into which we were thrown. ... Is this not strangely similar, however, to someone who proposes a universal theory of society and then, when he is criticized for not providing a link between this theory and his concrete social engagements, calmly replies that all our theoretical descriptions are overdetermined by the normative/descriptive complex in which we are implicated, and that, of course, the same goes for his own theory? What is missing here is simply the concrete elaboration of this link: if the theory of hegemony works as a description of the entire political process (and Laclau's most effective examples of the struggle for hegemony are often drawn from Fascism and other anti-democratic movements), *in what concrete way, then, is the normativity of radical democracy already at work in the theory of hegemony?* (And, incidentally, what makes this line of argument even more curious is its reliance on Heidegger who, from the same reference to the finite historical universe into which we are thrown as engaged agents, drew totally undemocratic political conclusions.)

The criticism can also be framed like this: what is the exact status of the reference to a specific historical moment in the sentence (quoted above) which asserts that the project of radical democracy is 'the result of a pluralization of social struggles anchored in the new structures of contemporary capitalism'? Does this mean that 'radical democracy' is *merely* the political project which fits today's constellation of pluralized struggles, while, in previous situations, other, more 'essentialist' and even undemocratic projects were appropriate? In this case, we would be back to the split between universal theory and particular forms of engagement: the theory of hegemony remains a universal abstract theory which explains why, today, radical democracy is the proper choice, while it also explains why, in a different situation, another choice would be more appropriate. If, however, the universal theory of hegemony is connected by a kind of umbilical cord to 'radical democracy', this, then, necessarily involves the pseudo-Hegelian historicist thesis that there are privileged historical moments which enable universal insight: today's situation of pluralized democratic struggles is such a moment which enables us to gain insight into the universal logic of the political. In 'Is There a Normative Deficit in the Theory of Hegemony?', Simon Critchley deals with this same problem:

[A]lthough the category of hegemony seems at one level to be a simple *description* of social and political life, a sort of value-neutral Foucauldian power-analytics, it is (and in my view has to be) a *normative* critique of much that passes for politics insofar as much politics tries to deny or render invisible its contingency and operations of power and force. . . . To push this a little further, we might say that only those societies that are self-conscious of their political status – their contingency and power operations – are democratic. What I mean is self-conscious at the level of the citizenry, not at the level of the Platonic Guardians, the Prince, or the latter's philosophical adviser. Machiavelli and Hobbes, it seems to me, were perfectly well aware of the contingency and political constitution of the social, but didn't exactly want this news broadcast to the people. Therefore, if all societies are *tacitly hegemonic*, then the distinguishing feature of democratic society is that it is *explicitly hegemonic*. Democracy is thus the name for that political form of society that makes explicit the contingency of its foundations. In democracy, political power is secured through operations of competition, persuasion and election based on the hegemonization of the 'empty place' that is the people, to use Claude Lefort's expression. Democracy is distinguished by the self-consciousness of the contingency of its operations of power; in extreme cases, by the self-consciousness of the very *mechanisms* of power.[12]

Critchley's way out of this predicament is to combine Laclau with a Derridean/Levinasian ethics of Otherness. However, is 'suturing', the 'essentialist' illusion, not a constitutive and irreducible part of every operation of hegemony? Is not 'hegemony' *effective* only on condition of its self-erasure? Is not the idea of a 'hegemony conscious of itself' an impossibility? In short, the usual deconstructive line of argument (showing how every essentialist

reference is already a 'sedimented' outcome of contingent decisions) has to be supplemented by its opposite: a minimum of
'naturalization' is a condition of effectiveness of the hegemonic
operation. This is clear from Laclau's non-Lacanian use of
'suture', its reduction to simple closure/fixation which is ultimately doomed to failure. 'Democratic' hegemony is thus
'hegemony under erasure', hegemony aware of its limited/failed
status – *je sais bien, mais quand même*. . . . This seems to indicate
that Laclau's theory of hegemony is ultimately a 'reflexive' theory, not a theory of political action but a theory of why every
action is haunted by an inner impossibility, and ultimately has to
fail. It is against this background that one can clearly perceive the
weakness of Laclau's recent diagnosis of the co-ordinates of
political struggle in Western democracies:

> . . . the Right and the Left are not fighting at the same level.
> On the one hand, there is an attempt by the Right to
> articulate various problems that people have into some kind
> of political imaginary, and on the other hand, there is a
> retreat by the Left into a purely moral discourse which
> doesn't enter into the hegemonic game. . . . The main dif-
> ficulty of the Left is that the fight today does not take place at
> that level of the political imaginary. And it relies on a
> rationalist discourse about rights, conceived in a purely
> abstract way without entering that hegemonic field, and
> without that engagement there is no possibility of a pro-
> gressive political alternative.[13]

Here we find the old Deleuzian theme, in all its naivety: as if the
main problem of the Left were its inability to propose a passionate

global vision of change. . . . Is it really that simple? Is the solution for the Left to abandon the 'purely moral' rationalist discourse, and propose a more engaged vision addressing the political Imaginary, a vision that could compete with the neoconservative projects and also with past leftist visions? Is not this diagnosis similar to the doctor's proverbial answer to the worried patient: 'What you need is a good doctor's advice!'? What about asking the elementary question: what, in concrete terms, would that new leftist vision *be*, with regard to its content? Is not the decline of the traditional Left, its retreat into the moral rationalist discourse which no longer enters the hegemonic game, conditioned by large-scale changes in the global economy over the last few decades – so where *is* a better leftist global solution to our present predicament to be found? The Third Way at least tried to propose a vision which took these changes into account. . . . The reasons for this ineffectiveness appear to be acknowledged in the same interview by Chantal Mouffe:

> I think this question of the radicalization of democracy involves the understanding that democracy is never going to be completely realized, but it is something which will always need to be a *project* which we are going to fight for, but knowing that we will never be able to reach it. I think it needs a transformation of people's understanding of their political action. People really need to be enthusiastic about political struggle and, at the same time, be aware that there is no final goal – *democracy is a process* which we are continually working towards. So we are clearly facing a difficulty in terms of the way passion can be mobilized.[14]

> I think, with respect to this question of socialism, it is interesting to note that the situation today is in a certain sense the reverse of the one when we wrote *Hegemony and Socialist Strategy*. When the book was published . . . we were arguing that the problem with the Left was that it was exclusively concerned with class struggles and the socialist aspect of the transformation of the relations of production. We suggested that the Left was not sensitive enough to other issues that were called the 'new social movements' or other forms of oppression. . . . I think that it is all right to fight against racism and sexism and all those issues, but one should not lose sight of the aspect of class.[15]

The problem with this formulation is that, in the postmodern 'anti-essentialist' discourse regarding the multitude of struggles, 'socialist' anti-capitalist struggle is posited as just one in a series of struggles ('class, sex and gender, ethnic identity' . . .), and what is happening today is not merely that the anti-capitalist struggle is getting stronger, but that it is once again assuming the central structuring role. The old narrative of postmodern politics was: from class essentialism to the multitude of struggles for identity; today, the trend is finally reversed. The first step is already accomplished: from the multitude of struggles for recognition to anti-capitalism; what lies ahead is the next, 'Leninist', step — towards politically organized anti-capitalism.

Linked to this weakness is that (*inter alia*, in his recent theorization of populism) Laclau relies all too unproblematically on the distinction between the ontological and the ontic, and it is precisely the political domain which displays the limitations of this distinction. In his critique of those who try to define populism at the level of its (ontic) content – in other words, with regard to the content of the positive terms to which the populist discourse refers (the 'people' itself) – Laclau asserts that populism can be properly conceived only at the purely formal ontological level, as the principle of articulation of the series of positive terms into a specific chain of equivalences. Against such formalism, one should assert an irreducible 'content' – not a naive positive content which would guarantee the unity of a notion, but a 'content' in the precise sense of some minimal ontic, purely contingent, remainder to which the very 'formal' ontological structure remains attached by a kind of umbilical cord.

Furthermore, the difference between Fascism and Communism is also 'formal-ontological', not simply ontic: it is not (as authors like Ernst Nolte claim) that we have in both cases the same formal antagonistic structure, where the place of the Enemy is merely filled in with a different positive element (class, race). In the case of race, we are dealing with a positive naturalized element (the presupposed organic unity of society is perturbed by the intrusion of the foreign body), while class antagonism is absolutely inherent to and constitutive of the social field. Fascism thus obfuscates antagonism, translating it into a conflict of positive opposed terms. In the same way, in psychoanalysis, sexual difference itself is elevated to 'ontological' status: it is not a mere ontic difference, but formal-structural difference in the symbolic horizon. [16] The same goes for the status of commodity fetishism in the Marxian 'critique of political economy': the young Lukács was the first to elevate it to the 'ontological' structure of modernity.

The proof that class struggle is not an ontic 'binary opposite' but a purely 'formal' transcendental gap is the fact that, *translated into positive terms*, it always involves *three*, not merely two elements – why? Because class struggle as antagonism is, as it were, its own obstacle, that which forever prevents *its own* direct expression, its translation into clear symbolic or positive terms. For that very reason, the characteristic feature of 'totalitarianisms' is that they try forcefully to translate the Three into the Two: Fascists and Nazis spoke of a 'plutocratic-Bolshevik plot', bringing together big capital and Communists, these two opposites, into One Enemy (embodied in the Jew, of course); liberals see Communism and Fascism as two modes of 'totalitarianism'; Stalinists themselves ultimately identify rightist and leftist deviations. In all these attempts, antagonism proper is translated into the opposition of two positive terms.

The way the term 'modernization' is used in the recent ideological offensive illustrates this structurally necessary 'complication': first, an abstract opposition is constructed between 'modernizers' (those who endorse global capitalism in all its aspects, from economic to cultural) and 'traditionalists' (those who resist globalization). Into this category of those who resist everything is then thrown, from traditional conservatives and the populist Right to the 'Old Left' (those who continue to advocate the welfare state, trade unions . . .). This categorization obviously does capture an aspect of social reality – recall the coalition of Church and trade unions which, in Germany in early 2003, prevented the legalization of Sunday opening for shops. It is not enough, however, to say that this 'cultural difference' traverses the entire social field, cutting across different strata and classes; it is not enough to say that this opposition can be combined in different ways with other oppositions (so that we can have conservative 'traditional value'-based resistance to global capitalist 'modernization', or moral conservatives who fully endorse capitalist globalization); in short, it is not enough to say that this 'cultural difference' is one in a series of antagonisms which are operative in today's social processes.

The failure of this opposition to function as the key to social totality does not only mean that it should be articulated with other differences. It means that it is 'abstract', and the wager of Marxism is that there is one antagonism ('class struggle') which overdetermines all the others and which is, as such, the 'concrete universal' of the entire field. The term 'overdetermination' is used here in its precise Althusserian sense: it does not mean that class struggle is the ultimate referent and horizon of meaning of all other struggles; it means that class struggle is the structuring principle which allows us to account for the very 'inconsistent' plurality of ways in which other antagonisms can be articulated into 'chains of equivalences'. For example, feminist struggle can be articulated into a chain with a progressive struggle for emancipation, or it can (and certainly does) function as an ideological tool of the upper-middle classes to assert their superiority over the 'patriarchal and intolerant' lower classes. And the point here is not only that the feminist struggle can be articulated in different ways with class antagonism, but that class antagonism is, as it were, doubly inscribed here: it is the specific constellation of the class struggle itself which explains why feminist struggle was appropriated by the upper-middle classes. (The same goes for racism: it is the dynamics of class struggle itself which explains why explicit racism is strong among the

SLAVOJ ŽIŽEK

lowest strata of white workers.) Here class struggle is the 'concrete universal' in the strict Hegelian sense: in relating to its
otherness (other antagonisms) it relates to itself, that is, it
(over)determines the way it relates to other struggles.

Why does Laclau avoid this step? It is crucial to note here how
Laclau's reference to Lacan is limited, and for structural reasons.
First, Laclau uses the term 'suture' in a naive way, to indicate
simply the impossible total closure; in Lacanian theory, 'suture' is
a much more complex notion standing for the paradoxical element which, within a given field, holds the place of its
constitutive Outside. Along these Lacanian lines, Badiou designates the 'nothing' or 'void' of a situation as its 'subtractive
suture to being':[17] far from enacting the closure of a situation,
suture introduces a gap which prevents its closure, a 'symptomal
torsion' embodied in the 'supernumerary' element which, while
it is part of the situation, has no place within it. More fundamentally, when Laclau talks about the 'object of desire', he is
referring simply to a fully realized Society, the impossible fullness
in which every dislocation would have been cancelled. It would
have been much more productive to introduce here the precise
Lacanian distinction between the object and the object-cause of
desire: the 'object' is the Thing, the impossible fullness of
Society, that which political agents desire; while the *cause* of
desire is a remainder, a 'partial object' – that, precisely, which
sticks out and disturbs the balance. The *cause* of desire in
democracy – its *objet petit a* – is the 'indivisible remainder', the
'pathological' partial object which resists being sublated [*aufge-
hoben*] in the contingent signifying game – for example, the
naturalized 'nation'.

102

'L'inconscient, c'est la politique'[18]

This brings us to the complex topic of 'Lacan and the political'. A series of interventions in 2003 approached the political implications of Lacan's theory in a new way; if we leave aside some directly conservative indications (like calls for the restoration of the 'strong' paternal Law as the only defence against the destructive potential of today's all-pervasive narcissim), the two main examples are Jacques-Alain Miller's turn towards 'psychoanalysis in the city' and Yannis Stavrakakis's attempt to link Laclau's and Mouffe's project of radical democracy to Lacan.

At this point, it is worth remembering that Miller started as an orthodox Maoist Althusserian; the gulf that separates his position in the late 1960s from his liberal-centrist platitudes of today is breathtaking.[19] The basic attitude is one of commonsense 'realistic' wisdom, which, of course, is ideology at its purest (elements of it are already discernible in Lacan himself): too much striving for purity can lead only to terrorism, so let us sensibly accept some degree of corruption. ... No wonder that the starting point of Miller's political considerations proper is the interest of psychoanalysis in the legal and social conditions of its own survival – therefore psychoanalysis advocates an independent civil society, political pluralism, a social life in which dissent and a sceptical attitude towards official ideals are tolerated. Psychoanalysis is subversive – it encourages distrust in all official ideals and institutions – but not revolutionary, since it also distrusts idealistic notions of a bright post-revolutionary future. What we encounter here is the old mantra about politics as the domain of identifications, ideals and Master-Signifiers, towards which one should maintain a sceptical

103

distance – political engagement turns us either into knaves or into fools. This underlying scepticism about progress is sustained by a somewhat elementary reference to the closure of libidinal economy: on the level of drives and their *jouissance*, there is no profit, since a gain on one level is always paid for by a loss on another.

No wonder Miller refers to Lacan's famous quip about political revolutions: at the end of the day, they always turn out to be revolutions in the original astronomical sense, that is to say, a circular move which brings us back to our starting point. (To pursue the celestial metaphor, however, does it not happen, from time to time, that a shift occurs in the very circular path of planetary revolutions, a break which redefines its co-ordinates and establishes a new balance or, rather, a new measure of balance?) On this basis, it is not difficult to guess what Miller's call for 'psychoanalysis in the city' amounts to – the following excerpt from a recent radio discussion is illuminating enough on this point:

> *Jacques-Alain Miller*: Present-day social life is enmeshed in such complex, abstract, impersonal networks that there is an effect of withdrawal into oneself, into what Michel Foucault called *le souci de soi*. Then people say: 'It's individualism, it's narcissism' – it's because the modern subject, the modern Frenchman, finds within himself, seeks within himself, an area of inner security. By this I mean that the trust you cannot find outside, you try to find within yourself. And that is why the contemporary ailment *par excellence* is depression. It is loss of self-confidence.
>
> Nowadays in France there is a feeling of insecurity. And it should be made clear that we are already living in a risk

society, with all the French nervousness which caused a number of revolutions in the nineteenth century – isn't that so? It can easily become a society of fear. And it, French society, is shot through by panic waves. They leave us . . .

Jean-Pierre Elkabbach: Well, Mr Psychoanalyst, what are the remedies?

Jacques-Alain Miller: Therefore it is easy to conclude: They leave us in the hands of quacks.

Jean-Pierre Elkabbach: Don't you believe that those who care should be distinguished from those who destroy? Those who do good to the individual, to the Frenchman I am, and those who do evil?

Jacques-Alain Miller: Of course.

Jean-Pierre Elkabbach: Because they're not competent, because they're not qualified, because they don't have the diplomas, because they don't have the experience.

Jacques-Alain Miller: Mr Elkabbach, don't try to create panic. The media bear a heavy responsibility here. It's very difficult for you to find the right balance between warning the public against problems, and most of all – most of all – not creating panic. . . . Analysts, psychoanalysts today, should be capable of conveying to the nation, to its representatives . . . a certain amount of knowledge they possess, and that could indeed deal with these panic waves which burst out periodically, which send decent people to court, including the High Court; and I would be glad if, from now on, a certain kind of discourse would change.[20]

When Freud, in his short essay on 'Fetishism', writes about the panic sparked off by the child's discovery of the absence of a penis in girls, he adds: 'The adult will later perhaps experience a similar panic when the cry goes up that the throne and the altar are in danger, and this panic will lead to similar illogical consequences.'[21] These consequences are, of course, the 'I know very well, but all the same' of fetishist denial – and is the main social function of the psychoanalyst really to 'prevent panic' by reassuring the public through collaboration with those in power? We cannot help being struck by the simplistic vulgarity of this underlying train of thought, which functions on the level of journalistic clichés mixed with some breathtaking curiosities (so the nineteenth-century French revolutions were caused by 'French nervousness'?): present-day social life is experienced as impenetrable and unpredictable; individuals lack the power of elementary cognitive mapping, which is why they either withdraw into themselves, to their inner life, or, if this defence strategy fails, get into a panic – and the analysts' duty is to help those in power to prevent these outbursts of panic (by reassuringly sustaining the appearances which mask the lack in the Other). The least one can say about Stavrakakis, in contrast to Miller, is that he is much more theoretically sophisticated – for that very reason, however, he reveals more clearly the conceptual frame that underlies Miller's ruminations: the short circuit between the assertion of ontological openness–contingency–undecidability, and democracy as the political form of this ontological openness. In a kind of political-ontological short circuit, democracy thus acquires a direct Lacanian legitimization as the 'politics of traversing the fantasy' – here, from a recent essay by Stavrakakis, is the model of this reasoning:

political attempts to realize modern utopian fantasies (notably the ideal of an Aryan Nazi order and that of a proletarian revolution leading to a future Communist society) have only reproduced a pattern typical of premodern eschatological discourses such as revolutionary millenarianism. The way all these discourses deal with negativity is more or less the following: Utopian fantasies promise to eliminate forever negativity in whatever sociopolitical form it takes. In order to achieve this impossible goal, utopian discourses *localize* the cause of negativity in one particular social group or political actor. . . . This historical argument can be supported by a *psychoanalytic argument*, regarding the function of fantasy in politics. From the point of view of a Lacanian ontology, fantasy . . . involves the dream of a state without disturbances and dislocations, a state in which we are supposed to get back the enjoyment sacrificed upon entering the symbolic order, while at the same time it relies on the production of a 'scapegoat' to be stigmatized as the one who is to blame for our lack, the *Evil* force that stole our precious *jouissance*. In order to sound credible in its promise to eliminate *negativity* it has to attribute to it a localized, 'controllable' cause (be it the Jews, the kulaks, etc.).

If this is the case, then surely one of the most urgent political tasks of our age is to traverse the fantasy of utopia and reinvent transformative politics in a post-fantasmatic direction. . . . Fortunately, it might not entail reinventing the wheel, it might not require a shift of Herculean proportions. One can encounter elements of such a political project in what is usually called the *democratic invention* or the *democratic revolution.* . . . No final resolutions are promised here, no political *Aufhebung*; antagonism is and remains constitutive. . . . The way radical democracy deals with negativity is by acknowledging its constitutive character and by assuming responsibility for its open, antagonistic administration, resisting at the same time the fantasy of its permanent resolution or its reduction into an advertising spectacle. In Lacanian terms, we can assert that radical democracy's deepening of the democratic revolution involves adopting an ethical position beyond the fantasy of harmony. It is here that the Lacanian ethics of psychoanalysis can lend support to a radical democratic project. [22]

This passage is worth quoting *in extenso*, since it presents, in a clear and concise way, the whole line of reasoning that we should question – everything is here, right up to the simplistic parallel between Nazism and Communism *à la* Ernst Nolte. The first thing that strikes us is the 'binary logic' on which Stavrakakis relies: on the one hand, in one big arch, premodern millenarian utopias, Communism and Nazism, which all imply the localization of the origin of Evil in a particular social agent (Jews, kulaks . . .) – once we have eliminated these 'thieves of (our) enjoyment', social harmony and transparency will be restored; on the other hand, the 'democratic invention', with its notion of the empty place of power, non-transparency and the irreducible contingency of social life, and so on. Furthermore, in so far as the utopia of a harmonious society is a kind of fantasy which conceals the structural 'lack in the Other' (irreducible social antagonism), and in so far as the aim of psychoanalytic treatment is to traverse the fantasy – that is to say, to make the analysand accept the non-existence of the big Other – is the radical democratic politics whose premises is that 'society doesn't exist' (Laclau) not *eo ipso* a post-fantasmatic politics?

There is a whole series of problems with this line of reasoning. First, in its rapid rejection of utopia, it leaves out of the picture the main utopia of today, which is the utopia of capitalism itself – it is Francis Fukuyama who is our true utopian. Second, it fails to distinguish between, on the one hand, the contingency and impenetrability of social life, and, on the other, the democratic logic of the empty place of power, with no agent who is 'naturally' entitled to it. It is easy to see how these two phenomena are independent of each other: if anything, a functioning democracy presupposes a basic stability and reliability of social life. Third, such a simplified binary opposition also ignores the distinction between the traditional functioning of power grounded in a 'naturalized' authority (king) and the millenarian radical utopia which strives to accomplish a radical rupture.

Is not Stavrakakis's dismissal of millenarian radicalism all too precipitate, overlooking the tremendous emancipatory potential of millenarian radicals, of their explosion of revolutionary nega-tivity? The very least we should do here is to complicate the picture by introducing two couples of opposites: first the oppo-sition full/empty place of power, then the opposition difference/antagonism as the fundamental structuring principle (to use Laclau's own terms). While the traditional hierarchical power presupposes a 'natural' bearer of power, it asserts difference (hierarchical social order) as the basic structural principle of social life, in contrast to millenarian 'fundamentalism', which asserts antagonism. On the other hand, democracy combines the assertion of contingency (the empty place of power) with difference: while it admits the irreducible character of social antagonisms, its goal is to transpose antagonisms into a regulated agonistic competition. So what about the fourth option: the combination of contingency and antagonism? In other words, what about the prospect of a radical social transformation which would not involve the well-worn scarecrow 'complete fullness and transparency of the social'? Why should every project of a radical social revolution automatically fall into the trap of aiming at the impossible dream of 'total transparency'?

As for Stavrakakis's fundamental operation, that of the identification with non-identity itself (the idea that 'democracy' functions as a paradoxical Master-Signifer of non-identity itself, that the democratic struggle is ultimately not the struggle for some specific positive content, but the struggle for a social order which incorporates contingency and openness themselves),[23] here Stavrakakis joins Miller, who develops the same theme with direct reference to Claude Lefort:

> Is 'democracy' a Master-Signifier? Without a doubt. It is the Master-Signifier which says that there is no Master-Signifier — at least, not a Master-Signifier which would stand alone; that every Master-Signifier has to insert itself wisely among others. Democracy is Lacan's big S of the barred A, which says: I am the signifier of the fact that the Other has a hole in it, or that it doesn't exist.[24]

Of course, Miller is aware that every Master-Signifier bears witness to the fact that there is no Master-Signifier, no Other of the Other; that there is a lack in the Other, and so on – the very gap between S_1 and S_2 exists because of this lack (like God in Spinoza, the Master-Signifier by definition fills in the gap in the series of 'ordinary' signifiers). The difference is that, in the case of democracy, this lack is directly inscribed into the social edifice, it is institutionalized in a set of procedures and regulations – no wonder, then, that Miller approvingly quotes Marcel Gauchet on how, in democracy, truth offers itself only 'in division and decomposition'. However, as an analyst, Miller perceives something Stavrakakis misses: he is aware of what radical democrats, in effect, 'do not see'. The democratic subject, which emerges through a violent abstraction from all its particular roots and determinations, is the Lacanian barred subject, $, which is as such foreign to – incompatible with – enjoyment:

> For us, democracy as empty place means: the subject of democracy is a barred subject. Our limited algebra enables us to grasp immediately that this leaves out the small *a*. That is to say: everything that hinges on the particularity of enjoyment. The empty barred subject of democracy finds it difficult to link itself to all that goes on, forms itself, trembles, in all that we designate with this comfortable small letter, the small *a*.
>
> We are told: once the empty place is there, everybody, if he respects the law, can bring in his traditions and his values. . . . However, what we know is that, in actual fact, the more democracy is empty, the more it is a desert of enjoyment, and, correlatively, the more enjoyment condenses itself in

certain elements. . . . The more the signifier is 'disaffected', as others have put it, the more the signifier is purified, the more it imposes itself in the pure form of law, of egalitarian democracy, of the globalization of the market . . . the more passion builds up, the more hatred intensifies, fundamentalisms proliferate, destruction spreads, massacres without precedents are carried out, and unheard-of catastrophes occur.[25]

This means that the democratic empty place and the discourse of totalitarian fullness are strictly correlative, two sides of the same coin: it is meaningless to play one against the other, and advocate a 'radical' democracy which would avoid this unpleasant supplement. So when Laclau and Mouffe complain that only the Right has the requisite passion, is able to propose a new mobilizing Imaginary, while the Left merely administers, what they fail to see is the structural necessity of what they perceive as a mere tactical weakness of the Left. No wonder the European project which is widely debated today fails to engage, to engender enthusiasm: it is ultimately a project of administration, not of ideological passion. The only passion is the rightist defence of Europe — all the leftist attempts to infuse the notion of united Europe with political passion (like the Habermas–Derrida initiative in summer 2003) fail to gain momentum. The reason for this failure is precisely the absence of the 'critique of political economy': the only way to account for the shifts described by Stavrakakis (the recent crisis of democracy, etc.) is to relate them to what goes on in contemporary capitalism. Both Laclau and Stavrakakis are, of course, aware of the link between 'democratic

invention' and totalitarianism – that is to say, they know that the
space for modern totalitarianism was opened up by democratic
invention itself. However, their standard formulation (in the style
of 'democratic invention brings new dangers and challenges, but
also new ways to mobilize the forces of democratic emancipation') misses the key point: that the 'fundamentalist' attachment
to *jouissance* is *the obverse, the fantasmatic supplement, of democracy
itself.*

There is a deeper historical problem with Miller's advocacy of
the 'subversive but not revolutionary' stance of psychoanalysis.
Think of his own claim[26] that in today's 'post-ideological' age,
when the stuff of politics is more and more directly the modes of
jouissance, the distribution and regulation of *jouissance* (abortion,
gay marriages, patriarchy . . .), psychoanalysis can no longer
maintain the old Freudian sceptical distance towards the public-
political domain: the gap between public and private is being
progressively abolished, *jouissance* is directly politicized. Does this
not entail that the sceptical stance of not taking social ideals and
identifications seriously is also no longer viable, since this scepticism is already the basic feature of the very hegemonic ideology
which no longer operates on the level of ideals and identifications,
but directly on the level of regulating *jouissance*?

Utopia and the Gentle Art of Killing

Thus the present crisis compels us to rethink democracy itself as
today's Master-Signifier. Democracy *qua* ideology functions
principally as the space of a virtual alternative: the very prospect
of a change in power, the looming possibility of this change,

makes us endure the existing power relations – that is to say, these existing relations are stabilized, rendered tolerable, by the false opening. (In a strict homology, subjects accept their economic situation if it is accompanied by an awareness of the possibility of change – 'good luck is just around the corner'.) The opponents of capitalist globalization like to emphasize the importance of keeping the dream alive: global capitalism is not the end of history, it is possible to think and act differently – what, however, if it is this very lure of a possible change which guarantees that nothing will actually change? What if it is only full acceptance of the desperate closure of the present global situation that can push us towards actual change? In this precise way, the virtual alternative displays an actuality of its own; in other words, it is a positive ontological constituent of the existing order.

'Democracy' is not merely the 'power of, by, and for the people'. It is not enough just to claim that, in a democracy, the will and interests (the two do not in any way automatically coincide) of the large majority determine the state's decisions. Democracy – in the way this term is used today – concerns, above all, formal legalism: its minimal definition is the unconditional adherence to a certain set of formal rules which guarantee that antagonisms are fully absorbed into the agonistic game. 'Democracy' means that, whatever electoral manipulation takes place, every political agent will unconditionally respect the results. In this sense, the US presidential elections of 2000 were effectively 'democratic': despite the obvious electoral manipulations, and the patent meaninglessness of the fact that a couple of hundred Florida votes decided who would be President, the Democratic candidate accepted his defeat. In the weeks of uncertainty after the elections, Bill Clinton made an appropriate acerbic comment: 'The American people have spoken; we just don't know what they said.' This comment should be taken more seriously than it was meant: even now, we do not know – maybe because there was no substantial 'message' behind the result at all.

Those who are old enough still remember the dull attempts of 'democratic socialists' to oppose the vision of authentic socialism to miserable 'really existing socialism' – to such an attempt, the standard Hegelian answer is quite adequate: the failure of reality to live up to its notion always bears witness to the inherent weakness of this notion itself. But why should the same not hold also for democracy itself? Is it also not all too simple to oppose to 'really existing' liberal capitalist democracy a more true 'radical' democracy?

Interestingly enough, there is at least one case in which formal democrats themselves (or, at least, a substantial number of them) would tolerate the suspension of democracy: what if formally free elections were won by an anti-democratic party whose platform promises the abolition of formal democracy? (This did happen in Algeria, among other places, a few of years ago.) In such a case, many a democrat would concede that the people were not yet 'mature' enough to be allowed democracy, and that some kind of enlightened despotism whose aim would be to educate the majority into becoming proper democrats was preferable. A crucial component of any populism is also the dismissal of the formal democratic procedure: even where these rules are still to be respected, it is always made clear that they do not provide the crucial legitimacy to political agents – populism, rather, evokes the direct pathetic link between the charismatic leadership and the crowd, verified through plebiscites and mass gatherings.

This is the sense in which one should render democracy problematic: why should the Left always and unconditionally respect
the formal democratic 'rules of the game'? Why should it not – in
some circumstances, at least – question the legitimacy of the
outcome of a formal democratic procedure? All democratic leftists venerate Rosa Luxemburg's famous 'Freedom is freedom for
those who think *differently.*' Perhaps the time has come to shift the
emphasis from 'differently' to 'think': 'Freedom is freedom for
those who *think* differently' – *only* for those who *really think*, even
if they think differently, not for those who just blindly
(unthinkingly) act out their opinions. In his famous short poem
'The Solution' (1953; published in 1956), Brecht mocked the
arrogance of the Communist *nomenklatura* in the face of the
workers' revolt:

> After the uprising of the 17th June
> The Secretary of the Writers Union
> Had leaflets distributed in the *Stalinallee*
> Stating that the people
> Had forfeited the confidence of the government
> And could win it back only
> By redoubled efforts.
> Would it not be easier
> In that case for the government
> To dissolve the people
> And elect another?[27]

This poem, however, is not only politically opportunistic, the obverse of his letter of solidarity with the East German Communist regime published in *Neues Deutschland* – to put it brutally, Brecht wanted to cover both flanks, to profess his support for the regime as well as to hint at his solidarity with the workers, so that whoever won, he would be on the winning side – but also simply *wrong* in the theoretico-political sense: one should openly admit that it really *is* a duty – even *the* duty – of a revolutionary party to 'dissolve the people and elect another', in other words, to bring about the transubstantiation of the 'old' opportunistic people (the inert 'crowd') into a revolutionary body aware of its historical tasks. Far from being an easy task, to 'dissolve the people and elect another' is the most difficult of all. . . . This means that one should take the risk of radically questioning today's predominant attitude of anti-authoritarian tolerance. Surprisingly, it was, Bernard Williams who, in his perspicacious reading of David Mamet's *Oleanna*, outlined the limits of this attitude:

A complaint constantly made by the female character is that she has made sacrifices to come to college, in order to learn something, to be told things that she did not know, but that she has been offered only a feeble permissiveness. She complains that her teacher . . . does not control or direct her enough: he does not tell her what to believe, or even, perhaps, what to ask. He does not exercise authority. At the same time, she complains that he exercises power over her. This might seem to be a muddle on her part, or the playwright's, but it is not. The male character has power over her (he can decide what grade she gets), but just because he lacks authority, this power is mere power, in part gender power.[28]

Power appears (is experienced) 'as such' at the very point where it is no longer covered by 'authority'. There are, however, further complications to Williams's view. First, 'authority' is not simply a direct property of the Master-figure, but an effect of the social relationship between the Master and his subjects: even were the Master to remain the same, it might happen that, because of the change in the socio-symbolic field, his position is no longer perceived as legitimate authority, but as mere illegitimate power (is not such a shift the most elementary gesture of feminism: male authority is suddenly unmasked as mere power?). The lesson of all revolutions from 1789 to 1989 is that such a disintegration of authority, its transformation into arbitrary power, always precedes a revolutionary outbreak. Where Williams is right is in his emphasis on how the very permissiveness of the power-figure, its self-restraint as regards exercising authority by directing and controlling his subject, results in that authority appearing as illegitimate power. Therein lies the vicious cycle of today's academe: the more professors renounce 'authoritarian' active teaching, imposing knowledge and values, the more they are experienced as figures of power. And, as every parent knows, the same goes for parental education: a father who exerts true transferential authority will never be experienced as 'oppressive' – on the contrary, it is, a father who tries to be permissive, who does not want to impose his views and values on his children, but allows them to find their own way, who is denounced as exerting power, as being 'oppressive'. . . .

The paradox to be fully endorsed here is that the only way to abolish power relations effectively leads through freely accepted relations of authority: the model of a free collective is not a group of libertines indulging their own pleasures, but an extremely disciplined revolutionary body. The injunction which holds such a collective together is best encapsulated by the logical form of the double negation (prohibition) which, precisely, is *not* the same as the direct positive assertion. Towards the end of Brecht's *Die Massnahme*, the Four Agitators declare:

> *It is a terrible thing to kill.*
> But not only others would we kill, but ourselves too if need be
> Since only force can alter this
> Murderous world, as
> Every living creature knows.
> It is still, we said
> Not given to us not to kill.[29]

The text does *not* say 'we are allowed to kill', but 'it is still not permitted [an adequate paraphrase of *vergönnen*] to us not to kill' – or, simply, it is still *prohibited* to us not to kill. Brecht's precision here is admirable: the double negation is crucial. 'We are permitted to kill' would amount to simple immoral permissiveness; 'we are ordered to kill' would transform killing into an obscene-perverse superego injunction that is the truth of the first version (as Lacan put it, the permitted *jouissance* inexorably turned into a prescribed one). The only correct formulation is thus the reversal of the biblical prohibition, the prohibition *not* to kill, which goes to the end, to the anti-Antigonean prohibition to provide for the proper funeral ritual: the young comrade has to 'vanish, and vanish entirely' – that is to say, his disappearance (death) itself should disappear, should not leave any (symbolic) trace. This radical stance is the logical conclusion of the self-erasure of the revolutionary agent who is denied not only public recognition but even posthumous recognition; in the 'Praise of Illegal Activity', the Control Chorus sings:

> Speaking, but
> Without betraying the speaker.
> Winning, but
> Without betraying the winner.
> Dying, but
> Without declaring the death.
> Who would not do a lot for fame? Who
> Would do as much for silence?[30]

This is revolutionary activity performed from the stance of 'subjective destitution': not 'authentically displaying one's position of enunciation', but erasing oneself behind the enunciated, in an act without a subject. What the immortal Martha Argerich said about her piano playing ('I love playing the piano, I just hate being a pianist') also goes for the revolutionary: she loves the revolution, but hates being a revolutionary.

Bernard Williams can again be of some help here, when he elaborates on what forever separates *must* from *ought*: '*Ought* is related to *must* as *best* is related to *only*.'[31] We arrive at what we must do after a long and anxious consideration of alternatives, and 'can have that belief while remaining uncertain about it, and still very clearly seeing the powerful merits of alternative courses'.[32] This difference between must and ought also relies on temporality: we can criticize somebody for not having done what he 'ought to have done', while we cannot say to someone: 'You must have done it' if he did not do it – we use the expression 'You had to do it' for consoling somebody who *did* a thing which he found distasteful (like 'Don't blame yourself – even if you do love him, you had to punish him!'), while the standard use of the expression 'You ought to have done it' implies, on the contrary, that you did *not* do it.

This reference to a 'must' also opens up the space of manipulation, as when a bargaining partner or outright blackmailer says that, 'deplorably', this leaves him with no alternative to an unpleasant course of action – and, we may add, like the ruthless Stalinist who 'cannot but' engage in terror. The falsity of this position lies in the fact that, when we 'must' do something, it is not only that, within the limits that our situation sets on our deliberation, we 'cannot do otherwise': the character of a person is revealed not only in the fact that he does what he must do, but also 'in the location of those limits, and in the very fact that one can determine, sometimes through deliberation itself, that one cannot do certain things, and must do others'.[33] And I *am* responsible for my character – that is, for the choice of co-ordinates which prevent me from doing some things and impel me to do others. This brings us to the Lacanian notion of the act: in an act, I precisely redefine the very co-ordinates of what I cannot and must do.

'Must' and 'Ought' thus relate to each other as the Real and the Symbolic: the Real of a drive whose injunction cannot be avoided (which is why Lacan says that the status of a drive is ethical); the Ought as a symbolic ideal caught in the dialectic of desire (if you ought not to do something, this very prohibition generates the desire to do it). When you 'must' do something, it means you have no choice but to do it, even if it is terrible: in Wagner's *Die Walküre*, Wotan is cornered by Fricka, and 'must' ('cannot but') allow the murder of Siegmund, although his heart bleeds for him; he 'must' ('cannot but') punish Brünnhilde, his dearest child, the embodiment of his own innermost striving. Incidentally, the same goes for Wagner's *Tristan und Isolde*, the Bayreuth staging of which was Heiner Müller's last great theatrical achievement: they *must*, they *cannot but*, indulge in their passion, even if this goes against their *Sollen*, their social obligations.

In Wotan's forced exercise of punishment, Wagner encounters the paradox of the 'killing with *pietà*' also at work in the Talmud (which calls on us to dispense Justice with Love) and in Brecht's two key *Lehrstücke, Der Jasager* and *Die Massnahme*, in which the young comrade is killed by his companions with loving tenderness. And this is something that today, in our epoch in which the abstract humanitarian rejection of violence is accompanied by its obscene double, anonymous killing *without pietà*, we need more than ever. Why, you may ask, is this?

The year 1990 – the year of the the collapse of Communism – is commonly perceived as the year of the collapse of political utopias: today, we live in a post-utopian time of pragmatic administration, since we learned the hard lesson of how noble political utopias end in totalitarian terror. . . . As I noted above, however, the first thing to remember here is that this alleged collapse of utopias was followed by the ten-year rule of the last grand utopia, the utopia of global capitalist liberal democracy as the 'end of history' – 9/11 designates the end of *this* utopia, a return to the real history of new walls of conflict which follow the collapse of the Berlin Wall. It is crucial to perceive how the 'end of utopia' repeated itself in a self-reflexive gesture: the ultimate utopia was the very notion that, after the end of utopias, we were at the 'end of history'.

The first thing to do here is to specify what we mean by utopia: in its essence, utopia has nothing to do with imagining an impossible ideal society; what characterizes utopia is literally the construction of a u-topic space, a social space outside the existing parameters, the parameters of what appears to be 'possible' in the existing social universe. The 'utopian' gesture is the gesture which changes the co-ordinates of the possible. That was the kernel of the Leninist 'utopia' which rose from the ashes of the catastrophe of 1914, in his settling of accounts with Second International orthodoxy: the radical imperative to smash the bourgeois state, which meant the state *as such*, and to invent a new communal social form without a standing army, police or bureaucracy, in which all could take part in the administration of social affairs. For Lenin, this was no theoretical project for some distant future – in October 1917, he claimed: 'we can at once set in motion a state apparatus constituted of ten if not twenty million people'.[34] *This urge of the moment is the true utopia.* What one should stick with is the *madness* (in the strict Kierkegaardian sense) of this Lenininst utopia – and, if anything, Stalinism stands for a return to realistic 'common sense'. It is impossible to overestimate the explosive potential of *The State and Revolution* – in this book, 'the vocabulary and grammar of the Western tradition of politics was abruptly dispensed with'.[35]

What this means is, again, that utopia has nothing to do with idle dreaming about ideal society in total abstraction from real life: 'utopia' is a matter of innermost urgency, something we are pushed into as a matter of survival, when it is no longer possible to go on within the parameters of the 'possible'. This utopia has to be opposed both to the standard notion of political utopias, books containing projects which were basically not even intended to be realized (from its first supreme case, Plato's *Republic*, up to Thomas More's *Utopia* and – not to be forgotten – De Sade's *Philosophy in the Boudoir*) and to what is usually referred to as the utopian practice of capitalism itself: commodities evoking utopian pleasures, the libidinal economy that relies on the dynamic of continuously generating new transgressive desires and practices, right up to necrophilia (think of the recent proposals to make corpses available to those who need them for their satisfaction).

And one of the strategies of utopia today resides in the aesthetic dimension. It is often claimed that, in his passionate advocacy of the aesthetic dimension as inherent to the political, Jacques Rancière nostalgically longs for the nineteenth-century populist rebellions whose time is definitively over. But is it really? Is not the 'postmodern' politics of resistance precisely permeated with aesthetic phenomena, from body-piercing and cross-dressing to public spectacles? Does not the curious phenomenon of 'flash mobs' represent aesthetico-political protest at its purest, reduced to its minimal frame? In flash mobs, people show up at an assigned place at a certain time, perform some brief (and usually trivial or ridiculous) acts, and then disperse again – no wonder flash mobs are described as urban poetry with no real purpose. Are these flash mobs not a kind of 'Malevich of politics', the political counterpart to the famous 'black square on white background', the act of marking a minimal difference?

Appendix II: *Lucus a non Lucendo*

Ethical Violence? Yes, please!

As I said above, today, in our era of oversensitivity with regard to 'harassment' by the Other, it is becoming increasingly common to complain about 'ethical violence' – that is, to submit to criticism ethical injunctions which 'terrorize' us with the brutal imposition of their universality. The (not so) secret model here is an 'ethics without violence', freely (re)negotiated – high-flying cultural critique unexpectedly meets lowly pop psychology. John Gray, author of *Men are from Mars, Women are from Venus*, deployed, in a series of Oprah Winfrey shows, a vulgarized version of narrativist-deconstructionist psychoanalysis: since we ultimately 'are' the stories we tell ourselves about ourselves, the solution to psychic deadlock lies in a creative 'positive' rewriting of the narrative of our past. What he had in mind was not only the standard cognitive therapy of changing negative 'false beliefs' about oneself into a more positive attitude of the assurance that one is loved by others and capable of creative achievements, but a more 'radical', pseudo-Freudian notion of regressing to the scene of the primordial traumatic wound. That is to say: Gray accepts the psychoanalytic notion of a hard kernel of some early-childhood traumatic experience that forever marks the subject's further development, giving it a pathological spin – what he proposes is that, after regressing to her primal traumatic scene, and thus directly confronting it, the subject should, under the therapist's guidance, 'rewrite' this scene, this ultimate phantasmatic framework of her subjectivity, in a more 'positive', benign

and productive narrative – if, for example, the primordial traumatic scene that became encrusted in your unconscious,
deforming and inhibiting your creative attitude, was that of your
father shouting at you: 'You are worthless! I despise you! Nothing
good will ever come of you!', you should rewrite it as a new
scene with a benevolent father smiling kindly at you and telling
you: 'You're OK! I have faith in you!' (In one Oprah Winfrey
show, Gray directly enacted this rewriting-the-past experience
with a woman who, at the end, gracefully embraced him, crying
with happiness, claiming that she was no longer haunted by her
father's contemptuous attitude towards her.) To play this game to
the end, when the Wolf Man 'regressed' to the traumatic scene
that determined his subsequent psychic development – witnessing
the parental *coitus a tergo* – the solution would have been to
rewrite this scene, so that what the Wolf Man actually saw was
merely his parents lying on the bed, his father reading a news-
paper and his mother a sentimental novel.

Ridiculous as this procedure may appear, let us not forget that
it also has its politically correct version, that of ethnic, sexual and
other minorities rewriting their past in a more positive, self-
assertive vein (African-Americans claiming that long before European modernity, ancient African empires already possessed
highly developed science and technology, and so forth). Along the
same lines, we can even imagine a rewriting of the Decalogue
itself: are not some of the Commandments just too severe? Let us
regress to the scene on Mount Sinai, and rewrite it: adultery –
yes, if it is sincere, and serves the goal of profound self-
realization. . . . What disappears in this total availability of the
past to its subsequent retroactive rewriting are not primarily the

'hard facts' but the Real of a traumatic encounter whose structuring role in the subject's psychic economy forever resists its symbolic rewriting.

The ultimate irony is that this 'critique of ethical violence' is sometimes even linked to the Nietzschean theme of moral norms as imposed by the weak on the strong, thwarting their life-assertiveness: 'moral sensitivity', bad conscience, feelings of guilt, as internalized resistance to the heroic assertion of Life. For Nietzsche, such 'moral sensitivity' culminates in the contemporary Last Man, who fears excessive intensity of life as something that may disturb his search for 'happiness' without stress, and who, for this very reason, rejects 'cruel' imposed moral norms as a threat to his fragile balance. What gets lost in this 'critique of ethical violence' is precisely the most precious and revolutionary aspect of the Jewish legacy. Let us not forget that, in the Jewish tradition, divine Mosaic Law is experienced as something externally and violently imposed, contingent and traumatic – in short, as an impossible/real Thing that 'makes the law'. What is arguably the ultimate scene of religious-ideological interpellation – the pronouncement of the Decalogue on Mount Sinai – is the very opposite of something that emerges 'organically' as the outcome of the path of self-knowledge and self-realization: the pronouncement of the Decalogue is *ethical violence at its purest*. The Judaeo-Christian tradition is thus to be strictly opposed to the New Age Gnostic problematic of self-realization or self-fulfilment: when the Old Testament enjoins you to love and respect your neighbour, this refers not to your imaginary *semblable*/double, but to the neighbour *qua* traumatic Thing. In contrast to the New Age attitude which ultimately reduces my

Other/Neighbour to my mirror-image, or to a means in my journey of self-realization (like Jungian psychology, in which other people around me are ultimately reduced to the externalizations/projections of different disavowed aspects of my personality), Judaism opens up a tradition in which an alien traumatic kernel forever persists in my Neighbour – the Neighbour remains an inert, impenetrable, enigmatic presence that hystericizes me.

The Jewish commandment which prohibits images of God is the obverse of the statement that relating to one's neighbour is the *only* terrain of religious practice, of where the divine dimension is present in our lives – the prohibition 'no images of God' does not point towards a Gnostic experience of the divine beyond our reality, a divine which is beyond any image; on the contrary, it designates a kind of ethical *hic Rhodus, hic salta*: you want to be religious? OK, prove it *here*, in 'works of love', in the way you relate to your neighbours. . . . This is a nice case of the Hegelian reversal of reflexive determination into determinate reflection: instead of saying 'God is love', we should say 'Love is divine' (and, of course, the point is not to conceive of this reversal as the standard humanist platitude). It is for this precise reason that Christianity, far from being a regression towards an image of God, merely draws the consequence of Jewish iconoclasm through asserting the identity of God and man.

If, then, the modern topic of human rights is ultimately grounded in this Jewish notion of the Neighbour as the abyss of Otherness, how did we reach the weird contemporary negative link between the Decalogue (the traumatically imposed divine Commandments) and human rights? That is to say: within our post-political liberal-permissive society, human rights are ultimately, in their essence, simply rights to violate the Ten Commandments. 'The right to privacy' = the right to adultery, done in secret, when no one sees me or has the right to probe into my private life. 'The right to pursue happiness and to possess private property' = the right to steal (to exploit others). 'Freedom of the press and of expression of opinion' = the right to lie. 'The right of free citizens to possess weapons' = the right to kill. And, ultimately, 'freedom of religious belief' = the right to worship false gods.[1] Of course, human rights do not directly condone the violation of the Commandments – the point is simply that they keep open a marginal 'grey zone' which remains out of reach of (religious or secular) power: in this shady zone, I can violate the Commandments, and if a power probes into it, catching me with my pants down, and tries to prevent my violations, I can cry: 'Assault on my basic human rights!' The point is thus that it is structurally impossible for Power to draw a clear line of separation and prevent only the 'misuse' of a right, while not infringing upon its proper use, that is, the use that does *not* violate the Commandments.

The first step in this direction was accomplished by the Christian notion of grace. In Mozart's *La Clemenza di Tito*, just before the final pardon, Tito himself expresses exasperation at the proliferation of treason which obliges him to multiply acts of clemency:

> The very moment that I absolve one criminal, I discover another. . . . I believe the stars conspire to oblige me, in spite of myself, to become cruel. No: they shall not have this

satisfaction. My virtue has already pledged itself to continue the contest. Let us see which is more constant, the treachery of others or my mercy. . . . Let it be known to Rome that I am the same and that I know all, absolve everyone, and forget everything.

One can almost hear Tito complaining: 'Uno per volta, per carità!' – 'Please, not so fast, one at a time in the mercy queue!' Living up to his task, Tito forgets everyone, but those whom he pardons are condemned to remember it for ever:

> *Sextus*: It is true, you pardon me, Emperor; but my heart will not absolve me; it will lament the error until it no longer has memory.
> *Titus*: The true repentance of which you are capable is worth more than constant fidelity.

This couplet from the finale blurts out the obscene secret of *clemenza*: the pardon does not really abolish the debt; rather, it makes it infinite – we are *for ever* indebted to the person who has pardoned us. No wonder Tito prefers repentance to fidelity: in fidelity to the Master, I follow him out of respect; while with repentance, what attaches me to the Master is infinite and indelible guilt. In this, Tito is a thoroughly Christian Master, the practitioner of a logic which culminates today in the new capitalist ethics, where the ruthless pursuit of profit is counteracted by charity: today, charity is part of the game as a humanitarian mask hiding underlying economic exploitation. In a superego-blackmail of gigantic proportions, the developed countries are constantly 'helping' the underdeveloped (with aid, loans, and so on), thereby avoiding the key issue – namely, their *complicity* in and co-responsibility for the miserable situation of the underdeveloped. Which discursive shift underlies this new form of domination?

The Four Discourses

Lacan provides the answer in *L'envers de la psychanalyse*, Seminar XVII (1969–70) on the four discourses, his response to the events of 1968. Its premise is best captured as his reversal of the well-known anti-structuralist graffito from the Paris walls of 1968 'Structures do not walk the streets!' if anything, this Seminar endeavours to demonstrate how structures *do* walk the streets: in other words, how structural shifts *can* account for social outbursts like that of 1968. Instead of one symbolic Order, with its set of a priori rules which guarantee social cohesion, we have the matrix of passages from one discourse to another: Lacan's interest is focused on the passage from the discourse of the Master to the discourse of the University as the hegemonic discourse in contemporary society. No wonder the revolt was located in the universities: as such, it merely indicated the shift to new forms of domination sustained and legitimized by the scientific discourse. Lacan's underlying premise is sceptical-conservative – his diagnosis is best captured by his famous retort to the student revolutionaries: 'As hysterics, you demand a new master. You will get one!' This passage can also be conceived in more general terms, as the passage from the pre-revolutionary *ancien régime* to the post-revolutionary new Master who does not want to admit that he is one, but puts himself forward as a mere 'servant' of the

People – in Nietzsche's terms, it is simply the passage from Master's ethics to slave morality, and this fact, perhaps, provides us with a new approach to Nietzsche: when Nietzsche scornfully dismisses 'slave morality', he is not attacking the lower classes as such but, rather, the new masters who are no longer ready to assume the title of Master – 'slave' is Nietzsche's term for a fake master.

The starting point of the matrix of the four discourses is Lacan's well-known 'definition' of the signifier: a signifier is that which 'represents the subject for another signifier' – how are we to read this obviously circular definition? The old-style hospital bed has at the foot, out of the patient's sight, a small display board on which different charts and documents are stuck, specifying the patient's temperature, blood pressure, medicines, and so on. This display represents the patient – for whom? Not simply and directly for other subjects (say, for the nurses and doctors who regularly check this panel), but primarily for other signifiers, for the symbolic network of medical knowledge in which the data on the panel have to be inserted in order to obtain their meaning. One can easily imagine a computerized system where the reading of the data on the panel proceeds automatically, so that what the doctor obtains and reads are not these data but directly the conclusions which, according to the system of medical knowledge, follow from these and other data. . . . The conclusion to be drawn from this definition of the signifier is that, in what I say, in my symbolic representation, there is always a kind of surplus with regard to the concrete, flesh-and-blood addressee(s) of my speech, which is why even a letter which fails to reach its concrete addressee *does* in a way arrive at its true destination, which is the big Other, the symbolic system of 'other signifiers'. One of the direct materializations of this excess is the symptom: a ciphered message whose addressee is not another human being (when I inscribe into my body a symptom which divulges the innermost secret of my desire, no human being is intended to read it directly), but which none the less has accomplished its function the moment it is produced, since it reached the big Other, its true addressee.[2]

Lacan's schema of the four discourses articulates the four subjective positions within a discursive social bond which logically follow from the formula of the signifier (which is why psychosis is excluded: it designates the very breakdown of the symbolic social bond). The whole construction is based on the phenomenon of the symbolic *reduplicatio*, the redoubling of an entity into itself and the place it occupies in the structure, as in Mallarmé's *rien n'aura eu lieu que le lieu*, or Malevich's black square on a white background, both displaying an effort to formulate place as such or, rather, the minimal difference between the place and an element which precedes the difference between elements. *Reduplicatio* means that an element never 'fits' its place: I am never fully what my symbolic mandate tells me I am. For that reason, the discourse of the Master is the necessary starting point, in so far as in it an entity and its place *do* coincide: the Master-Signifier effectively occupies the place of the 'agent', which is that of the Master; the *objet petit a* occupies the place of 'production', which is that of unassimilable excess, and so forth. And it is the redoubling, the gap between the element and the place, which then sets the process in motion: a Master hystericizes himself by starting to question what actually makes him a Master, and on it goes.

So, on the basis of the discourse of the Master, one can then proceed to generate the three other discourses by successively putting the other three elements in the place of the Master: in the University discourse, it is Knowledge which occupies the agent's (Master's) place, turning the subject ($) into that which is 'produced', into its unassimilable excess–remainder; in hysteria, the true 'Master', the agent who, in effect, terrorizes the Master himself, is the hysterical subject, with her incessant questioning of the Master's position. So, first, the discourse of the Master provides the basic matrix: a subject is represented by the signifier for another signifier (for the chain or the field of 'ordinary' signifiers); the remainder – the 'bone in the throat' – which resists this symbolic representation emerges (is 'produced') as the *objet petit a*, and the subject endeavours to 'normalize' his relationship towards this excess via phantasmatic formations (which is why the lower level of the formula of the Master's discourse renders the matheme of fantasy $\$ - a$). In apparent contradiction to this determination, Lacan often claims that the discourse of the Master is the only discourse which excludes the dimension of fantasy – how are we to understand this? The illusion of the gesture of the Master is the complete coincidence between the level of enunciation (the subjective position from which I am speaking) and the level of the enunciated content – that is to say, what characterizes the Master is a speech act which wholly absorbs me, in which 'I am what I say'. In short, the Master's speech functions as a fully self-contained performative.

Such an ideal coincidence, of course, precludes the dimension of fantasy, since fantasy emerges precisely in order to fill in the gap between the enunciated content and its underlying position of enunciation: fantasy is an answer to the question 'You are telling me all this, but why? What do you really want to achieve by telling me this?' The fact that the dimension of fantasy none the less persists thus simply indicates the ultimate unavoidable failure of the Master's discourse. Suffice it to recall the proverbial high-flying manager who, from time to time, feels compelled to visit prostitutes in order to engage in masochistic rituals where he is 'treated as a mere object': the semblance of his active public existence, in which he gives orders to his subordinates and runs their lives (the upper level of the Master's discourse, S_1–S_2), is sustained by the fantasies of being turned into a passive object of another's enjoyment (the lower level: \$ – a). In Kant's philo-sophy, the faculty of desire is 'pathological', dependent on contingent objects, so there can be no 'pure faculty of desire', no 'critique of pure desire'; while for Lacan, psychoanalysis precisely *is* a kind of 'critique of *pure* desire'. In other words, desire *does* have a non-pathological ('a priori') object-cause: the *objet petit a*, the object which overlaps with its own lack.

What is a Master-Signifier? In the very last pages of his monumental *The Second World War*, Winston Churchill ponders on the enigma of a political decision: after the specialists (economic and military analysts, psychologists, meteorologists . . .) have supplied their multiple, elaborate and refined analysis, somebody must take on the simple and, for that very reason, most difficult act of transposing this complex multitude – where for every reason for, there are two reasons against, and vice versa – into a simple 'Yes' or 'No': we shall attack; we shall continue to wait.

... This gesture, which can never be fully grounded in reasons, is that of a Master. The Master's discourse thus relies on the gap between S_2 and S_1, between the chain of 'ordinary' signifiers and the 'excessive' Master-Signifier. Take military ranks – the curious fact that they do not overlap with the position within the military hierarchy of command: from the rank of an officer – lieutenant, colonel, general – one cannot directly derive a person's place in the hierarchical chain of command (battalion commander; commander of an army group). Originally, of course, ranks were directly grounded in a certain position of command – however, the curious fact is precisely the way they came to redouble the designation of this position, so that today one says 'General Michael Rose, commander of the UNPROFOR forces in Bosnia'. Why this redoubling – why do we not abolish ranks, and simply designate an officer by his or her position in the chain of command? Only the Chinese Army in the heyday of the Cultural Revolution abolished ranks and simply used position in the chain of command. The necessity of redoubling is the necessity of adding a Master-Signifier to the 'ordinary' signifier which designates one's place in the social hierarchy. This same gap is also exemplified by the two names of the same person. The Pope is simultaneously Karol Wojtyla and John Paul II: the first name stands for the 'real' person, while the second name designates this same person as the 'infallible' embodiment of the Institution of the Catholic Church – while poor Karol can get drunk and babble stupidities, when John Paul speaks, it is the divine spirit itself which speaks through him.

We can now see in what precise sense we are to understand Lacan's thesis according to which what is 'primordially repressed' is the binary signifier (that of *Vorstellungs-Repräsentanz*): what the symbolic order precludes is the full harmonious presence of the couple of Master-Signifiers, S_1–S_2 as *yin–yang* or any other two symmetrical 'fundamental principles'. The fact that 'there is no sexual relationship' means precisely that the secondary signifier (that of the Woman) is 'primordially repressed', and what we get in the place of this repression, what fills in its gap, is the multitude of 'returns of the repressed', the series of 'ordinary' signifiers. In Woody Allen's Tolstoy parody *Love and Death*, the first association that automatically comes to mind, of course, is: 'If Tolstoy, where is Dostoevsky?' In the film, Dostoevsky (the 'binary signifier' to Tolstoy) remains 'repressed' the price of this, however, is that a conversation in the middle of the film includes the titles of all Dostoevsky's main novels: 'Is that man still in the underground?' 'You mean one of the Karamazov brothers?' 'Yes, that idiot!' 'Well, he did commit his crime and was punished for it!' 'I know, he was a gambler who always risked too much!', and so on. Here we encounter the 'return of the repressed', that is to say, the series of signifiers which fills in the gap of the repressed binary signifier 'Dostoevsky'. This is why the standard deconstructionist criticism according to which Lacan's theory of sexual difference falls into the trap of 'binary logic' totally misses the point: Lacan's *la femme n'existe pas* aims precisely at undermining the 'binary' polar couple of Masculine and Feminine – the original split is not between the One and the Other, but is strictly inherent to the One; it is the split between the One and its empty place of inscription (this is how we should read Kafka's famous statement that the Messiah will come one day after his arrival). This is also how we should think of the link between the split inherent to the One and the explosion of the multiple: the multiple is not the primordial ontological fact; the 'transcendental' genesis of the multiple resides in the lack of the binary signifier – that is to say, the multiple emerges as the series of attempts to fill in the gap of the missing binary signifier.

Thus there is no reason to be dismissive of the discourse of the Master, to identify it too hastily with 'authoritarian repression': the Master's gesture is the founding gesture of every social bond. Let us imagine a confused situation of social disintegration, in which the cohesive power of ideology has lost its efficiency: in such a situation, the Master would be the one who invented a new signifier, the famous 'quilting point', which again stabilized the situation and made it readable; the University discourse, which would then elaborate the network of Knowledge which sustained this readability, would by definition presuppose and rely on the initial gesture of the Master. The Master adds no new positive content; he merely adds a signifier which suddenly turns disorder into order – into 'new harmony', as Rimbaud would have put it. Let us take as an example anti-Semitism in Germany in the 1920s: people felt disorientated, succumbing to an undeserved military defeat, an economic crisis which ate away at their life savings, political inefficiency, moral degeneration . . . and the Nazis provided a single agent which accounted for it all: the Jew, the Jewish plot. That is the magic of a Master: although there is nothing new at the level of positive content, 'nothing is quite the same' after he pronounces his Word.

Thus the difference between S_1 and S_2 is not the difference of two opposed poles within the same field but, rather, the cut within this field – the cut of the level at which the process occurs

– inherent to the one term. Topologically, we get the same term at two surfaces. In other terms, the original couple is not that of two signifiers, but that of the signifier and its *reduplicatio* – that is, the minimal difference between a signifier and the place of its inscription, between one and zero. How, then, do S_1 and S_2 relate? We oscillate between two opposed versions: in the first version, the binary signifier, the symmetrical counterpart of S_1, is 'primordially repressed', and it is in order to supplement the void of this repression that the chain of S_2 emerges – or, to put it another way, the original fact is the couple of S_1 and the Void at the place of its counterpart, and the chain of S_2 is secondary; in the second version, in the account of the emergence of S_1 as the 'enigmatic term', the empty signifier, the primordial fact is, on the contrary, S_2, the signifying chain in its incompleteness, and it is in order to fill in the void of this incompleteness that S_1 intervenes. How are the two versions to be co-ordinated? Is the ultimate fact the vicious circle of their mutual implication?

The University discourse is enunciated from the position of 'neutral' Knowledge; it addresses the remainder of the real (say, in the case of pedagogical knowledge, the 'raw, uneducated child'), turning it into the subject ($). The 'truth' of the University discourse, hidden beneath the bar, of course, is power, or the Master-Signifier: the constitutive lie of the University discourse is that it disavows its performative dimension, presenting what effectively amounts to a political decision based on power as a simple insight into the factual state of things. What one should avoid here is the Foucauldian misreading: the produced subject is not simply the subjectivity which arises as a result of the disciplinary application of power–knowledge, but its remainder, that which eludes the grasp of power–knowledge. 'Production' (the fourth term in the matrix of discourses) does not stand simply for the result of the discursive operation but, rather, for its 'indivisible remainder', for the excess which resists being included in the discursive network – that is to say, for what the discourse itself produces as the foreign body at its very heart.

Perhaps the exemplary case of the Master's position which underlies the University discourse is the way in which medical discourse functions in our everyday lives: at the surface level, we are dealing with pure objective knowledge which desubjectivizes the subject–patient, reducing her to an object of research, of diagnosis and treatment; underneath, however, one can easily discern a worried hystericized subject, obsessed with anxiety, addressing the doctor as her Master and asking for reassurance from him. (And I am tempted to claim that doctors' resistance to being treated just like other scientists stems from their awareness that their position is still that of the Master, which is why we do not expect the doctor just to tell us the unvarnished (objective) truth: he is expected to tell us the bad news only in so far as our knowledge of our serious condition will somehow help us to cope with it – if it would only make things worse, he is expected to withhold it from the patient.)[3] At a more common level, we should merely recall the market expert who advocates strong budgetary measures (cutting welfare expenditure, and so forth) as a necessity imposed by her neutral expertise free of any ideological bias: what he conceals is the series of power relations (from the active role of state apparatuses to ideological beliefs) which sustain the 'neutral' functioning of the market mechanism.

In the hysterical link, the $ over *a* stands for the subject who is divided, traumatized, by what kind of object she is for the Other, what role she plays in the Other's desire: 'Why am I what you're saying that I am?', or, to quote Shakespeare's Juliet, 'Why am I that name?' This, for Lacan, is the primordial situation of a small child, thrown into a spider's web of libidinal investments: she is somehow aware of being the focus of the libidinal investments of others, but cannot grasp *what* it is that these others see in her – what she expects from the Other–Master is knowledge about what she is as object (the lower level of the formula). The protagonist of Racine's *Phèdre* is hysterical in so far as she resists the role of object of exchange between men by incestuously violating the proper order of generations (falling in love with her stepson). Her passion for Hyppolite aims not at its direct realization–satisfaction but, rather, at the very act of its confession to Hyppolite, who is thus forced to play the double role of Phèdre's object of desire and of her symbolic Other (the addressee to whom she confesses her desire). When Hyppolite learns from Phèdre that he is the cause of her consuming passion, he is shocked – this knowledge possesses a clear 'castratory' dimension; it hystericizes him: 'Why me? What kind of object am I to have this effect on her? What does she see in me?' What produces the unbearable castrating effect is not the fact of being deprived of 'it' (the *agalma*, the object-cause of desire) but, on the contrary, the fact of clearly 'possessing it': the hysteric is horrified at being 'reduced to an object', that is to say, at being invested with the *agalma* which makes him or her the object of another's desire.

Unlike the hysteric, the pervert knows perfectly well what she is for the Other: a knowledge supports his position as the object of the Other's (divided subject's) *jouissance*. For that reason, the, formula of the discourse of perversion is the same as that of the analyst's discourse: Lacan defines perversion as the inverted fantasy – that is to say, his formula of perversion is $a - \$$, which is precisely the upper level of the analyst's discourse. The difference between the social bond of perversion and that of analysis is grounded in the radical ambiguity in Lacan of *objet petit a*, which stands simultaneously for the imaginary phantasmatic lure/screen and for that which this lure is obfuscating: for the Void behind the lure.

So, when we pass from perversion to the analytic social bond, the agent (analyst) reduces herself to the void which provokes the subject into confronting the truth of her desire. Knowledge in the position of 'truth' below the bar under the 'agent', of course, refers to the supposed knowledge of the analyst, and, simultaneously, indicates that the knowledge gained here will be not the neutral 'objective' knowledge of scientific adequacy, but the knowledge which concerns the subject (analysand) in the truth of her subjective position. In this precise sense, what the discourse of the analyst 'produces' is the Master-Signifier, the 'swerve' of the patient's knowledge, the surplus element which situates the patient's knowledge at the level of truth: after the Master-Signifier is produced, even if nothing changes at the level of knowledge, the 'same' knowledge as before starts to function in a different mode. The Master-Signifier is the unconscious *sinthome*, the cipher of enjoyment, to which the subject was unknowingly subjected.

The crucial point not to be missed here is how this identification of the analyst's subjective position as that of *objet petit a* in Lacan's late work functions as an act of radical self-criticism:

earlier, in the 1950s, Lacan had conceived the analyst not as the small other (a) but, on the contrary, as a kind of stand-in for the big Other (A, the anonymous symbolic order). At this level, the analyst's function was to frustrate the subject's imaginary misrecognitions, and make her accept her proper symbolic place within the circuit of symbolic exchange, the place which effectively (and unbeknown to her) determines her symbolic identity. Later, however, the analyst stands precisely for the ultimate inconsistency and failure of the big Other – that is, for the symbolic order's inability to guarantee the subject's symbolic identity.

So, if a political Leader says, 'I am your Master; let my will be done!', this direct assertion of authority is hystericized when the subject starts to doubt his qualification to act as a Leader ('Am I really their Master? What is it in me that legitimizes me to act like that?'); it can be masked in the guise of the University discourse ('In asking you to do this, I am merely guided by insight into objective historical necessity, so I am not your Leader, merely your servant who enables you to act for your own good . . .'); or the subject can act as a blank, suspending her symbolic efficiency and thus compelling her Other to become aware of how she was experiencing another subject as a Leader only because she was treating him as one.

It should be clear, from this brief description, how the position of 'agent' in each of the four discourses involves a specific mode of subjectivity: the Master is the subject who is fully engaged in his (speech) act, who, in a way, 'is his word', whose word displays an immediate performative efficiency; the agent of the University discourse is, on the contrary, fundamentally disengaged: she posits herself as the self-effacing observer (and executor) of 'objective laws' accessible to neutral knowledge (in clinical terms, her position is closest to that of the pervert). The hysterical subject is the subject whose very existence involves radical doubt and questioning; her entire being is sustained by the uncertainty as to what she is for the Other; in so far as the subject exists only as an answer to the enigma of the Other's desire, the hysterical subject is the subject *par excellence*. Again, in clear contrast to this, the analyst stands for the paradox of the desubjectivized subject, of the subject who fully assumes what Lacan calls 'subjective destitution', that is, who breaks out of the vicious cycle of the intersubjective dialectics of desire, and turns into an acephalous being of pure drive.

A Cup of Decaffeinated Reality

As for the political reading of this matrix, this is how each of the discourses clearly designates a political bond: the Master's discourse is the elementary mode of political authority sustained by fantasy; the University discourse is the rule of post-political 'experts'; hysterical discourse is the logic of protest and 'resistance', of demands which, according to Lacan's formula, really want to be rejected because *'ce n'est pas ça'* (because, if it is fully granted, the literal satisfaction of the demand robs it of its metaphorical universal dimension – the demand for X was not 'really about X'); the analyst's discourse is radical revolutionary-emancipatory politics in which the agent is *a*, the symptomal point, the 'part of no part', of the situation, with knowledge in the place of truth (that is, articulating the agent's position of enunciation and thus regaining the explosive effect of truth), $ the addressee of the agent, the ex-Master who is now hystericized, since the agent questions his position by 'producing', deploying openly, explicating as such, the Master-Signifier, and thus rendering it inoperable (as in the paradox of the 'states which are essentially by-products': once it is questioned, authority loses its self-evidence). How, then, within this frame, are we to read the University discourse more closely?

$$\frac{S_2}{S_1} \qquad \frac{a}{\$}$$

In the University discourse, is not the upper level ($ – a) that of *biopolitics* (in the sense deployed from Foucault to Agamben)? That of expert knowledge dealing with its object, which is a – not subjects, but individuals reduced to bare subsistence? And does not the lower level of the formula designate what Eric Santner has called the 'crisis of investiture', or the impossibility of the subject's relating to S_1, of identifying with a Master-Signifier, or of assuming the imposed symbolic mandate?[4] The usual notion of the relationship between surplus-enjoyment and symbolic identification is that symbolic identity is what we get in exchange for being deprived of enjoyment; what happens in contemporary society, with the decline of the Master-Signifier and the rise of consumerism, is the exact obverse: the basic fact is the loss of symbolic identity, Santner's 'crisis of investiture', and in exchange for this loss we are bombarded from all sides with forms and gadgets of enjoyment.

The Real Cancún (2003), the first ever 'reality movie', follows sixteen people together over eight days in a beachfront Cancún villa for the ultimate spring-break vacation. The movie, which was advertised as having 'NO SCRIPTS. NO ACTORS. NO RULES. ANYTHING CAN HAPPEN ON SPRING BREAK, AND IT DID', fared rather poorly at the box office (earning less than $4 million). It is easy to see why, in contrast to the triumph of the TV reality shows, it failed: the attempt to 'let life itself write the story' ended up in a mass of material out of which the studio experts tried to concoct a short coherent narrative. More important than such specific criticisms, however, is the insight into the ideological background which made such a film possible and acceptable.

From the 1950s onwards, social psychology has played endless variations on the theme of how, in public life, we all 'wear masks', adopt identities which obfuscate our true selves. However, wearing a mask can be a strange thing: sometimes, more often than we tend to believe, there is more truth in the mask than there is in what we assume to be our 'real self'. Think of the proverbial impotent shy person who, while playing a cyberspace interactive game, adopts the screen identity of a sadistic murderer and irresistible seducer – it is all too easy to say that this identity is just an imaginary supplement, a temporary escape from his real-life impotence. The point is, rather, that since he knows that the cyberspace interactive game is 'just a game', he can 'show his true self', do things he would never do in real-life interactions – in the guise of a fiction, the truth about himself is articulated.

The negative aspect of this wearing of a mask is the strange prohibition which until recently ruled hard-core pornography: although it showed 'everything', real sex, the narrative which provided the frame for repeated sexual encounters was, as a rule, ridiculously non-realistic, stereotypical, stupidly comical, staging a kind of return to eighteenth-century *commedia dell 'arte* in which actors do not play 'real' individuals, but one-dimensional types – the Miser, the Cuckolded Husband, the Promiscuous Wife. Is not this strange compulsion to make the narrative ridiculous a kind of negative gesture of respect: yes, we do show everything, but precisely for that reason we want to make it clear that it is all a big joke, that the actors are not really involved?

Today, however, this 'No trespass!' is increasingly undermined: recall recent attempts to combine 'serious' narrative cinema with the 'hardcore' depiction of sex – that is, to include in a 'serious' film sex scenes which are played for real (we see the erect penis, fellatio, and so on, up to and including actual penetration); the two most conspicuous examples are Patrice Chéreau's *Intimacy* and Lars von Trier's *Idiots*. And I would suggest that the rise of 'reality TV' in its different guises, from 'docusoaps' to *Survivor* competition shows, relies on the same underlying trend of obfuscating the line that separates fiction from reality. What are the ideological co-ordinates that underlie this trend?

These co-ordinates allow us to delineate succinctly what is false in reality TV shows: the 'real life' we get in them is as real as decaffeinated coffee. In short, even if these shows are 'for real', people are still acting in them – they simply *play themselves*. The standard disclaimer in a novel ('All the characters in this book are fictitious, and any resemblance to actual persons, living or dead, is purely coincidental') also holds for participants in reality soaps: what we see there are fictitious characters, even if they play themselves for real. The best comment on reality TV is thus the ironic version of this disclaimer recently used by a Slovene author: 'All the characters in the following narrative are fictitious, not real – but so are the characters of most of the people I know in real life, so this disclaimer doesn't amount to much . . .'. So, back to *The Real Cancún*: 'NO SCRIPTS. NO ACTORS. NO RULES' turned out to mean that people played themselves, that they abided by the most banal rules of social interaction, and that nothing even minimally unpredictable happened.

The key point here is that the expert rule of 'biopolitics' is grounded in and conditioned by the crisis of investiture; this crisis generated the 'post-metaphysical' survivalist stance of the Last Men, which ends up in an anaemic spectacle of life dragging on as its own shadow. Another aspect of the same shift is the rise of the term 'ideology' in the very epoch of the dissolution of the hegemonic role of the Master's discourse. In its classic Althusserian formulation, ideology is characterized in terms of the interpellation by the Master-Signifier, that is, as a version of the discourse of the Master; however, the term 'ideology' dates back to the late Napoleonic period – in other words, to the very historical moment when the Master's discourse started to lose its hold; we should therefore say that we started to talk about 'ideology' at the very point when ideology started to lose its immediate 'natural' character, and to be experienced as something artificial, no longer substantial but, precisely, 'mere ideology'. The same applies to the Oedipus complex, whose very theorization by Freud was conditioned by the crisis and decline of Oedipus in social reality.

The 'object' of the discourse of the University, however, has two aspects which cannot but seem to belong to two opposed ideological spaces: that of the reduction of humans to bare sub-sistence, to *Homo sacer* as the disposable object of expert knowledge; and that of respect for the vulnerable Other taken to an extreme, of the attitude of narcissistic subjectivity which experiences itself as vulnerable, constantly exposed to a multitude of potential 'harassments'. Is there a stronger contrast than the one between respect for the Other's vulnerability and the reduction of the Other to 'mere life' regulated by administrative knowledge? But what if these two stances none the less stem from the same root; what if they are two aspects of one and the same underlying attitude; what if they coincide in what I would des-ignate as the contemporary case of the Hegelian 'infinite judgement' which asserts the identity of opposites? What the two poles share is precisely the underlying refusal of any higher Causes, the notion that the ultimate goal of our lives is life itself. Nowhere is the complicity of these two levels clearer than in the case of opposition to the death penalty – this is not surprising, since (violently putting another human being to) death is, quite logically, the ultimate traumatic point of biopolitics, the politics of the administration of life. To put it in Foucauldian terms: is not the abolition of the death penalty part of a certain 'biopolitics' which considers crime to be the result of social, psychological, ideological, and so forth, circumstances: the notion of the morally/legally responsible subject is an ideological fiction whose function is to cover up the network of power relations, indivi-duals are not responsible for the crimes they commit, so they should not be punished? Is not the obverse of this thesis, however, that those who control the circumstances control the people? No wonder the two strongest industrial complexes today are the military and the medical, that of destroying and that of prolonging life.

The ultimate example of this ambiguity is arguably the *chocolate laxative* available in the USA, with the paradoxical injunction: 'Do you have constipation? Eat more of this chocolate!' – in other words, of the very thing which causes constipation. We find here a weird version of Wagner's famous 'Only the spear which caused the wound can heal it' from *Parsifal*. And is not a negative proof of the hegemony of this stance the fact that real unconstrained consumption (in all its main forms: drugs, limitless sex, smoking, eating . . .) is emerging as the main danger? The fight against these dangers is one of the main features of contemporary 'biopolitics'. Solutions are desperately sought which would reproduce the paradox of the chocolate laxative. The main contender is 'safe sex' – a term which makes us appreciate the truth of the old saying: 'Isn't having sex with a condom like taking a shower with your raincoat on?' The ultimate goal would be here, along the lines of decaffeinated coffee, to invent 'opium without opium': perhaps this is why marijuana is so popular among liberals who want to legalize it – it already *is* a kind of 'opium without opium'.

And we cannot avoid this deadlock by distinguishing 'common' hedonism from allegedly 'higher' spiritual self-fulfilment. The lesson of the recent events in Bhutan, the model for Shangri-la, is very instructive here. In 1998, the Dragon King of Bhutan defined his nation's guiding principle as Gross National Happiness: the idea being that, as a country ruled by spirituality, Bhutan should reject the Western materialist principle of Gross National Product as the measure of the success of society's development, and, rather, let itself be guided by the quest for true spiritual happiness. Debates about the definition of happiness ensued: a delegation from the Foreign Ministry, sent abroad to investigate whether happiness could be measured, finally found a Dutch professor who, after lifelong research, had reached the conclusion that happiness equals $10,000 a year, the minimum on which one can live comfortably. . . . The problem, of course, is that of the very concept of 'Gross National Happiness': what one can measure in one way or another is its opposite, a 'Net National Happiness' defined in precise positive quantified terms, and the gap which separates the two is filled in by what Lacan called *objet petit a*, the object-cause of desire which can disturb any direct correlation between (Net) Happiness and actual happiness. It is this 'factor X' which accounts for the strange result of a recent opinion poll in which a large sample of citizens of different countries was asked how happy they felt: the highest score was reached in Bangladesh, a poor overpopulated country which suffers catastrophic floods every year, and the lowest score in Germany, one of the few countries with surviving welfare-state mechanisms and one of the usual contenders for top position in the competition for the highest 'quality of life'.[5] This does not mean that one should renounce universality in politics, endorsing the 'deep' insight into how there are no universal standards – in Kantian terms, the conclusion should simply be that one should not search for universality at the level of 'pathological' (contingent and contextually dependent) notions such as 'happiness'.

The structure of the 'chocolate laxative', of a product containing the agent of its own containment, can be discerned throughout today's ideological landscape. There are two topics which determine today's tolerant liberal attitude towards others: respect for otherness, openness towards it, *and* obsessive fear of harassment – in short, the other is all right in so far as its presence is not intrusive, in so far as the other is not really other. . . . In strict analogy with the paradoxical structure of the chocolate laxative, tolerance thus coincides with its opposite: my duty to be tolerant towards the other effectively means that I should not get too close to her, or intrude into her space – in short, that I should respect her *intolerance* towards my overproximity. This is what is increasingly emerging as the central 'human right' in late-capitalist society: *the right not to be 'harassed'*, that is, to be kept at a safe distance from others. A similar structure is clearly present in the way we relate to capitalist profiteering: it is acceptable *if* it is counteracted with charitable activities – first you amass billions, then you return (part of) them to the needy. The same goes for war, for the emergent logic of humanitarian or pacifist militarism: war is permissible in so far as it really serves to bring about peace and democracy, or to create conditions for distributing humanitarian help. The same holds increasingly even for democracy and human rights: human rights are to be defended if they are 'rethought' in order to include torture and a permanent state of emergency; democracy is a good thing if it is cleansed of its populist 'excesses' and limited to those who are 'mature' enough to practise it.[6]

This same structure of the chocolate laxative is also what makes a figure like George Soros ethically so repulsive: does he not stand for the most ruthless financial speculative exploitation combined with its counter-agent, humanitarian concern about the catastrophic social consequences of the unbridled market economy?

Soros's very daily routine is an embodied lie: half of his working time is devoted to financial speculation, and the other half to 'humanitarian' activities (providing finance for cultural and democratic activities in post-Communist countries, writing essays and books) which ultimately combat the effects of his own speculation. Figures such as Soros are ideologically much more dangerous than crude direct market profiteers – this is where one should be truly Leninist, that is, react like Lenin when he heard a fellow Bolshevik praising a good priest who sincerely sympathized with the plight of the poor. Lenin retorted that what the Bolsheviks needed were priests who got drunk, robbed the peasants of the last remnants of their meagre resources, and raped their wives – for they made the peasants clearly aware of what priests in fact were, while the 'good' priests only confused this insight.

A conference on 'Fighting Terrorism for Humanity: A Conference on the Roots of Evil', which took place in New York on 22 September 2003, was the result of an initiative by the Prime Minister of Norway, Kjell Magne Bondevik, and the Nobel Peace Prize Laureate Professor Elie Wiesel; it was organized by the International Peace Academy and the Norwegian Mission to the UN, and held at the Inter-Continental/Barclay Hotel. The purpose of the conference was

> to help distinguish the real roots and origins of terrorism from factors that have a weaker link with terror and to discuss new policy measures in the global campaign against terrorism. Focusing on the true causes will enable us to fight terrorism more effectively. We need to identify the breeding grounds and the origins of hate in order to eliminate them,

and we need to formulate medium- and long-term policies in addition to the immediate action we have adopted to protect citizens and prevent these crimes.

What looked especially promising was the third session of this conference, the 'Round Table of World Leaders' who were invited to comment on the findings of the Oslo conference and other sources of knowledge about the causes of terrorist acts; as the official programme specified, after this session '[t]here will be a closed lunch for participants at the Round Table of World Leaders. Aides, experts and other participants will be invited to a buffet lunch.' They ate, making us throw up   how can we not recall here Brecht's acerbic fable about the origins of the Frankfurt School: in his old age, a rich capitalist, haunted by pangs of bad conscience, dedicated a large sum of money to a group of wise men, and charged them with finding the origins of misery and suffering in the world – forgetting the fact that he himself was this origin. The sources of Evil discussing the roots of Evil. . . .

When one talks about biopolitics, however, one should be careful to note that the category of 'pure (or mere) life' has nothing whatsoever to do with any biological or experiential immediacy – it is thoroughly determined by its symbolic context. Two different examples may clarify this point. A cereal pack is a (symbolic) envelope containing the reality of cereals – an envelope which contains the expiry date which determines the way we perceive the reality of cereals. Think of the horror we feel when we discover that we are already past that date: all of a sudden, we perceive *the same* cereal which a minute ago appeared to promise healthy pleasure as a suspicious, potentially harmful

substance. Here, the Real (the *objet petit a*) is that invisible X in the object whose presence or absence decides whether what I see is a delicious meal or a threat to my health, even if in reality the thing looks exactly the same. In a different context, when King Hussein of Jordan was already 'clinically dead' in February 1999 (his internal organs had ceased to function, and he was kept alive only by machines that regulated his heartbeat), his death (disconnection from the machine that kept his heart beating) was postponed until proper preparations had been made for the orderly transfer of power – is this not a nice case of the distinction 'between the two deaths'?

This brings us to the link between S_2 and the agency of the superego: the superego is not directly S_2; it is, rather, the S_1 of the S_2 itself, the dimension of an unconditional injunction that is inherent to knowledge itself. Take the health warnings we are bombarded with all the time: 'Smoking is dangerous!' 'Too much fat may cause a heart attack!' 'Regular exercise means a longer life!', and so on – it is impossible not to hear as an undertone the unconditional superego injunction 'You must enjoy a long and healthy life!' ... Hegel successfully resisted this danger: his theory of monarchy is the ultimate proof that he occupied a unique position between the discourses of the Master and that of the University: while rejecting the abolition of the Master, aware of the necessity of the Master's exceptional position as safeguard against the terror of Knowledge, he no longer succumbed to its charisma, but reduced it to the stupidity of an empty signifying function.

The modern Master justifies himself through his expert knowledge: one does not become a Master through birth, or mere symbolic investiture; rather, one has to earn the position through education and qualifications – in this simple and literal sense, modern power is knowledge, is grounded in knowledge. The passage from Master's discourse to University discourse means that the state itself emerges as the new Master: the state is run by the expertise of qualified bureaucrats. And Hegel, from his position in the midst of this shift, was able to perceive what remains hidden before and after, as is clear from his deduction of the necessity of the monarch in a rational state – a monarch reduced to a pure signifying function, deprived of any actual power. Hegel was thus aware of the necessity to maintain the gap between S_1 and S_2: if this gap gets obliterated, the result is 'totalitarian' bureaucracy as S_2.

The University discourse as the hegemonic discourse of modernity has two forms of existence in which its inner tension ('contradiction') is externalized: capitalism, with its logic of the integrated excess, of the system reproducing itself through constant self-revolutionizing; and bureaucratic 'totalitarianism', which is conceptualized in different guises as the rule of technology, of instrumental reason, of biopolitics, as the 'administered world'. How, precisely, do these two aspects relate to each other? We should not succumb to the temptation of reducing capitalism to a mere form of appearance of the more fundamental ontological fact of technological domination; rather, we should insist, in the Marxian mode, that the capitalist logic of integrating surplus into the functioning of the system is the fundamental fact. Stalinist 'totalitarianism' was the capitalist logic of self-propelling productivity liberated from its capitalist form, which is why it failed: Stalinism was the symptom of capitalism.

Stalinism involved the matrix of the *general intellect*, of the planned transparency of social life, of total productive mobilization – and its violent purges and paranoia were a kind of a 'return of the repressed', the 'irrationality' inherent to the project of a totally organized 'administered' society.

This means that the two levels, precisely in so far as they are two sides of the same coin, are ultimately incompatible: there is no meta-language enabling us to translate the logic of domination back into capitalist reproduction-through-excess, or vice versa. What, then, is the way out of this predicament? How do we break the circle of this mutual implication? Perhaps we should begin with an elementary insight. A lot of contemporary claims that the twentieth century was the most catastrophic in the whole of human history, the lowest point of nihilism, the situation of most extreme danger, and so on, forget the elementary lesson of dialectics: the twentieth century appears as such because the criteria themselves have changed – today, we simply have much higher standards of what constitutes violation of human rights. The fact that the situation appears catastrophic is thus, in itself, a positive sign, a sign of (some kind of) progress: today we are much more sensitive to the things which were going on also in previous epochs. Take feminism: only for the last two hundred years has the situation of women been progressively perceived as unjust, although it was 'objectively' getting better. Or the treatment of disabled individuals: even a couple of decades ago, the special entrances to restaurants, theatres, and so forth, which enable them to have access would have been unthinkable.

Innocent Violence

The way out none the less involves violence – but of what kind? When Carl Schmitt deployed his theory of the state of exception as a reply to Walter Benjamin's 'critique of violence', what he wanted to abolish was Benjamin's idea of a 'pure' extra-legal violence wholly external to the law (that is, revolutionary violence), as opposed to both law-positing violence and law-enforcing (or law-maintaining) violence. Schmitt wanted to achieve two things: to contain the horror of 'pure' violence, that is, to locate a place *within* the edifice of the law for the very violent suspension of the law; *and* to maintain a *distance* between the state of exception and the 'normal' rule of law, to prevent conflation of the two (the state of exception is the founding exception with regard to the universal rule of law). Against Schmitt, Benjamin insisted that, precisely, today (in the twentieth-century political context), we are less and less able to distinguish the two: the 'state of exception' is progressively turning into the normal state; and the necessary consequence of this overlapping is that we have to have recourse to what Benjamin calls the 'actual [*wirkliches*] state of exception', 'pure' revolutionary violence, as opposed to the state of exception whose aim is precisely to contain this threat and to guarantee that 'things will get back to normal', so that 'order will again prevail' (all rightist *coups d'état*, from Chile to Turkey, always invoked this need for things to get back to normal, for the 'madness of universal politicization to stop', so that people could return to work).[7]

Giorgio Agamben has developed in detail this theme of how the state of exception (the suspension of the rule of law on behalf of the law itself) generates as its object pure life – in both its aspects. In other words, it gives the sovereign power the right to dispense with the life of its subjects without any limitations, thereby turning states into killing machines, and simultaneously defining 'biopolitics' as the core of politics (measures destined to improve the health of the population – already in Hitler's Germany there was an abundance of regulations and advice concerning proper food, from wholewheat bread onwards). It is an ironic confirmation of Hitler's status as a 'biopolitician' that one of the first executive measures he issued after taking power in 1933 concerned the protection of life – the prohibition of the sacrificial slaughter of animals (aimed, of course, at Jewish rituals). We are thus confronted with the co-dependence of the two sides, the pure tautological exercise of power grounded only in itself – the rule of a 'pure' law which suspends all positive particular laws (in Lacanese: S_1) – and 'pure' life as its object (in Lacanese: a). These two excesses, the excess of law over all particular positive laws and the excess of pure life over all citizens' determinations, are the two sides of the same coin – what disappears in this process is simply politics as such, for biopolitics is, at its core, post-politics.

Here we must supplement these three forms of violence thematized by Benjamin ('pure' violence, the law-founding violence of the state of exception, and the law-maintaining violence of the 'normal' state) with 'simple' criminal violence against which the law-maintaining violence (re)acts. The symmetry is clear here: just as law-maintaining violence tries to contain 'simple' criminal violence, law-founding violence tries to contain 'pure' revolutionary violence; it is a reaction to its threat.

Is not Agamben's topic of the state of exception as simultaneously internal and external to the (rule of) Law best formulated with reference to Lacan's 'formulae of sexuation'? The paradox of the 'state of exception' (of the suspension of the legal order justified by the need to prevent chaos and maintain the rule of law) is that of what Lacan called '*extimité* [extimacy]'. Schmitt's insistence on the distance between the 'normal' rule of law and the state of exception which grounds it follows the logic of the 'masculine' side of Lacan's formulae of sexuation: the universal (rule of law) grounded in its constitutive exception. And is not Benjamin aiming precisely to counteract it with the 'feminine' side: the rule of law is 'non-all', that is to say, not everything is subject to the rule of law, precisely because there is no exception, no outside to the law to ground its universality. It is in this direction that, perhaps, one should look for the answer to the difficult key question: how to imagine 'pure' violence outside the law. Just as 'pure life' is not simply external to the rule of law, but generated by the self-referring suspension of the rule of law on behalf of the law itself (so that, in a Hegelian way, one can claim that 'pure life' is identical to – is the speculative equivalent of – 'pure' law), 'pure violence' is also strictly internal to the law – it simply involves a different mode of its self-relation. What one should accomplish is the passage from pure life to pure violence.

Maybe one of the figures of the law deprived of the force of normativity, the law with which one can play freely, would be the specifically Jewish attitude embodied in Kafka's work. Remember, in Kafka's *The Trial*, the discussion between Josef K. and the priest after (and about) the parable of the Door of the Law: what cannot fail to strike us is the totally non-initiatic, non-mystical, purely 'external', pedantically legal nature of this discussion. In these unsurpassable pages, Kafka practises the unique Jewish art of reading as the manipulation of the signifier, of the 'dead letter', best expressed by the commentators' motto quoted by the priest: 'The right perception of any matter and a misunderstanding of the same matter do not wholly exclude each other.' Suffice it to mention the priest's claim that the really deluded person in the parable is not the man from the country, but the doorkeeper himself who 'is subject to the man and does not know it'. But why? A bondsman is always subject to a free man, and it is obviously the man from the country who is free: he can go wherever he likes, he came to the Door of the Law of his own free will, while the doorkeeper is bound to his post. Since the door was meant only for the man from the country, the door-keeper had to be waiting there for years for the man from the country's whimsical decision to go to the Door of the Law – can we imagine a starker contrast to the ecstatic obscurantist her-meneutics looking for secret spiritual messages? There is no mystical Secret that we are approaching here, no Grail to be uncovered, just dry bureaucratic haggling – which, of course, makes the whole procedure all the more uncanny and enigmatic.

The same goes for 'real-life' Jewish practice. The standard Christian criticism is that the Jews, by searching for ways to obey God's commandments and prohibitions literally, and none the less going on doing as they please, effectively cheat Him. (There is a religious institution in Israel which deals specifically with issues of how to circumvent the prohibitions; significantly enough, it is called The Institute for Judaism and Science.) This criticism is meaningful within the confines of the standard Christian attitude whereby what matters is the spirit, not the letter – in other words, you are guilty if the desire was in your heart, even if in deed you did not break any letter of the law. When, in order not to break the injunction that no pigs should be raised on the holy land of Israel, pigs are raised on plateaus three feet above the ground (in a kibbutz north of Tel Aviv), the Christian interpretation would be: 'See how hypocritical the Jews are! The meaning of their God's command is clear – just don't raise pigs! And the Jews, in a typically hypocritical way, take the divine statement *literally*, focusing on the totally unimportant specification ''on the holy land of Israel'', and thus find a way of violating the spirit of the injunction while keeping to its letter. . . . For us Christians, they are already guilty in their heart, because they spent all their energy not on internalizing God's prohibition, but on how they can have their cake and eat it, on how they can circumvent the prohibition.' This, however, is *not* how one should read the Jewish attitude: there is no secret obscene transgression in it, no 'Ha-ha, we've cheated God by obeying Him literally'. What we should strive to regain today is this absolute hermeneutic naivety which, paradoxically, coincides with extreme cunning – with a cunning which is the very opposite of the cunning celebrated today, the cunning of noble lies and bitter truths.

Of Noble Lies and Bitter Truths

In a TV interview, Ralf Dahrendorf linked the growing distrust in democracy to the fact that, after every revolutionary change, the road to new prosperity leads through a 'vale of tears': after the breakdown of socialism, one cannot pass directly to the abundance of a successful market economy – the limited, but real, socialist welfare and social security systems have to be dismantled, and these first steps are necessarily painful; the same goes for Western Europe, where the passage from the post-World War II welfare state to the new global economy involves painful renunciations, less social security, less guaranteed social care. For Dahrendorf, the problem is best encapsulated by the simple fact that this painful passage through the 'vale of tears' lasts longer than the average period between (democratic) elections, so that the temptation to postpone difficult changes for short-term electoral gain is great. For him, the paradigmatic constellation here is the disappointment of large strata of post-Communist nations with the economic results of the new democratic order: in the glorious days of 1989, they equated democracy with the abundance of Western consumerist societies; now, more than ten years later, when this abundance is still lacking, they blame democracy itself. Unfortunately, he focuses much less on the opposite temptation: if the majority resists the necessary structural changes in the economy, would one of the logical conclusions not be that, for a decade or so, an enlightened elite should take power, even by non-democratic means, to enforce the necessary measures, and thus to lay the foundations for a truly stable democracy? Along these lines, Fareed Zakaria points out how democracy can 'catch on' only in economically developed countries: if developing countries are 'prematurely democratized', the result is a populism which ends in economic catastrophe and political despotism – no wonder today's economically most successful Third World countries (Taiwan, South

Korea, Chile) embraced full democracy only after a period of authoritarian rule.

This inherent crisis of democracy is also the reason for the renewed popularity of Leo Strauss: the key feature which makes his political thought relevant today is the elitist notion of democracy, that is, the idea of a 'noble lie', of how elites should rule, aware of the actual state of things (the brutal materialist logic of power, and so forth), while feeding the people fables which keep them satisfied in their blessed ignorance. For Strauss, the lesson of the trial and execution of Socrates is that Socrates was guilty as charged: philosophy *is* a threat to society. By questioning the gods and the ethos of the city, philosophy undermines the citizens' loyalty, and thus the basis of normal social life. Yet philosophy is also the highest, the worthiest, of all human endeavours. The resolution of this conflict was that the philosophers should – and in fact did – keep their teachings secret, passing them on by the esoteric art of writing 'between the lines'. The true, hidden message contained in the 'Great Tradition' of philosophy, from Plato to Hobbes and Locke, is that there are no gods, that morality is unfounded prejudice and that society is not grounded in nature.

But does Strauss's notion of esoteric knowledge not confuse two different phenomena: the cynicism of power, its unreadiness to admit publicly its own true foundations, and the subversive insights of those who aim at undermining the power system? For example, under Really Existing Socialism, there was a difference between a critical intellectual who, in order to get his message across, had to hide it in the terms of official ideology, and the cynical high-ranking member of the *nomenklatura* who was aware of the falsity of the basic claims of the ruling ideology. Or, in Christianity, there is an abyss which separates a Renaissance atheist trying to pass his message on in a coded way from the Renaissance pope making fun of Christian belief at a private orgy. Recall the passage from Roudinesco quoted above, directed against those who perceive gay communities as the model of totalitarian collectives which exclude otherness:

> For now, the only apocalypse that seems to threaten Western society – and Islam as well – is radical Islamic fundament- alism disposed to terrorism. Islamic threats are made by extremist bearded and barbaric polygamists who constrain women's bodies and spit invectives against homosexuals, whom they hold responsible for weakening the masculine values of God the father.[8]

However, does this clear demarcation not miss the inherent complexity of the situation? As everyone who had to do military service knows, brutal homophobia can easily coexist (and usually *does* coexist) with thwarted latent homosexuality. That is to say, why does the army universe so strongly resist publicly accepting gays into its ranks? Not because homosexuality poses a threat to the alleged 'phallic and patriarchal' libidinal economy of the army community, but, on the contrary, because the libidinal economy of the army community itself relies on a thwarted/disavowed homosexuality as the key component of the soldiers' male bonding. As I have had occasion to mention before, from my own experience I remember how the old infamous Yugoslav People's Army was homophobic to an extreme (when someone was discovered to have homosexual inclinations, he was instantly turned into a pariah, treated as a non-person, before being formally dismissed from the Army), yet, at the same time, everyday army life was excessively permeated with an atmosphere of homosexual innuendo. For example, when soldiers were queuing for their meal, a common vulgar joke was to stick a finger into the anus of the person in front of you and then to withdraw it quickly, so that when the surprised person turned round, he did not know who, among the soldiers behind him sharing a stupid obscene smile, was the actual perpetrator. The key point not to be missed here is how this fragile coexistence of extreme and violent homophobia with a thwarted – that is, publicly non-acknowledged – 'underground' homosexual libidinal economy bears witness to the fact that the discourse of the military community can be operative only by censoring its own libidinal foundation.

When Strauss talks about the necessity, for a philosopher, of employing 'noble lies' – that is, resorting to myth, to narratives *ad captum vulgi* – he does not draw all the consequences from the ambiguity of this stance, torn between the idea that wise philosophers know the truth, but judge it inappropriate for the common people, who cannot bear it (the direct knowledge of truth would undermine the very foundations of their morality, which needs the 'noble lies' of a personal God who punishes sins and rewards good deeds), and the idea that the core of truth is inaccessible to conceptual knowledge as such, which is why philosophers themselves have to resort to myths and other forms of fabulation to fill in the structural gaps in their knowledge. Strauss is, of course, aware of the ambiguity of the status of a secret: a secret is not only what the teacher knows but refrains from divulging to the non-initiated – a secret is also a secret for the teacher himself, something that he himself cannot fully penetrate and articulate in conceptual terms. Consequently, a philosopher uses parabolic and enigmatic speech for two reasons: in order to conceal the true core of his teaching from the common people, who are not ready for it; and because such a speech is the only way to describe the highest philosophical content.[9] As Hegel would have put it, the secrets of the Egyptians (for us) were secrets also for the Egyptians themselves.

No wonder, then, that Strauss answers in a properly Hegelian way the commonsensical criticism according to which, when we get the esoteric explanation of a work which is already in itself esoteric (like, say, Maimonides' reading of the Bible), such an explanation will be twice as esoteric and, consequently, twice as difficult to understand as is the esoteric text itself:

thanks to Maimonides, the secret teaching is accessible to us in two different versions: in the original Biblical version, and in the derivative version of [Maimonides'] *Guide*. Each version by itself might be wholly incomprehensible; but we may become able to decipher both by using the light which one sheds on the other. Our position resembles then that of an archaeologist confronted with an inscription in an unknown language, who subsequently discovers another inscription reproducing the translation of that text into another unknown language. ... [Maimonides] wrote the *Guide* according to the rules which he was wont to follow in reading the Bible. Therefore, if we wish to understand the *Guide*, we must read it according to the rules which

Maimonides applies in that work to the explanation of the Bible.[10]

The redoubling of the problem thus paradoxically generates its own solution. We should bear in mind here that, when Strauss is emphasizing the difference between exoteric and esoteric teaching, he conceives of this opposition in a way which is almost the exact opposite of today's New Age propagation of esoteric wisdom: the content of New Age wisdom is some kind of spiritual higher reality accessible only to the initiated few, while common mortals see around them only vulgar reality; for Strauss, on the contrary, and in a properly dialectical way, such narratives of a spiritual mystery would have been the very model of fables concocted *ad captum vulgi*. Is not this status of 'spiritual mysteries' confirmed by the success of the recent wave of religious thrillers epitomized by Dan Brown's *The Da Vinci Code*? These thrillers are perhaps the best indicator of today's ideological shift: the hero is in search of an old manuscript which would reveal some shattering secret that threatens to undermine the very foundations of (institutionalized) Christianity; the 'criminal' edge is provided by the desperate and ruthless attempts of the Church (or some hardline faction within it) to suppress this document. This secret as a rule focuses on the 'repressed' feminine dimension of the divine: Christ was married to Mary Magdalene; the Grail is actually the female body; or other variations. The paradox to be grasped here is that it is *only* through the 'monotheistic' suspension of the feminine signifier, of the polarity of masculine and feminine opposites, that the space emerges for what we broadly refer to as 'feminism' proper, for the rise of feminine subjectivity (which ultimately coincides with subjectivity as such).

In contrast to this tendency, for Strauss, the unbearable esoteric secret is the fact that there is no God and no immortal soul, no divine justice; that there is only this terrestrial world, with no deeper meaning and no guarantee of a happy outcome of ethical struggles.

When Strauss deploys the inherent paradox of a theology which proceeds *ad captum vulgi*, he provides a textbook case of the Hegelian 'negation of negation'.[11] In the first step, Spinoza asserts that, in the Bible, God speaks the language of ordinary people, adapting His speech to vulgar prejudices (presenting Himself as a wise lawgiver who performs miracles, utters prophecies and dispenses mercy) – in short, He tells stories which mobilize the resources of human imagination. In the second step, however, the question necessarily poses itself: is the idea of a God as a supreme Person who employs ruses, displays mercy and rage, and so on, not in itself a common idea which can occur only when one speaks 'with a view to the capacities of the vulgar masses'?

From the Freudian perspective, the key strategy of the 'art of writing' under conditions of persecution is that of *repetition*: when a writer apparently just repeats or recapitulates a content he previously deployed or took from a classical text, the clues are small, barely discernible, changes in the repeated content – a feature added, a feature left out, a changed order of features.[12] Here Strauss follows literally Freud's advice that, when the patient repeats the narrative of a dream, the small changes he introduces into the second version provide the key to its interpretation – in order to arrive at the core of a dream, one should focus not on what remains the same in its different versions, but precisely on minor changes. (And does the same not hold for Wagner's great retrospective narratives from his *Ring*, in which we hear yet again what happened in previous operas, in previous acts of the same opera, or in the past before the events staged in the opera(s)? Here also, the small changes in the retelling provide the key.)

The perfect example of Strauss's 'art of writing' under conditions of persecution is the fate of the human sciences (especially philosophy) under Stalinism. Soviet philosophy, at least from the late 1940s onwards, was by no means a monolithic dogmatic edifice: intense struggles were going on all the time, but since, in order to get published, all philosophers had to pay lip service to dialectical materialism, and quote Marx–Engels–Lenin–Stalin, the only way to detect them was through a Straussian reading – all the strategies enumerated by Strauss were there: selective repetition of known theses; proposing a thesis whose implication is a negation of an official thesis; deliberate self-contradictions; up to the all-too-convincing presentation of a view that one officially condemns (the notorious chapters on 'contemporary bourgeois philosophy'). And is not the same Straussian logic silently advocated also by outspoken critics of biogenetic interventions? The secret knowledge here is that man is just a neuronal machine whose innermost properties could be manipulated – were these insights publicly asserted, however, they would undermine the foundations of our ethical subjective stance, and thus cause a global ethical crisis; it is therefore better to keep them secret, as esoteric knowledge which should not be propagated, so that ordinary people will maintain a minimum of morality.

Hegel can also be read in a Straussian way: when he emphasizes how society – the existing social order – is the ultimate space in which the subject finds his substantial content and recognition – in other words, how subjective freedom can actualize itself only in the rationality of the universal ethical order – the implied (albeit not explicitly stated) obverse is that those who do *not* find this recognition also have the right to rebel: if a class of people are systematically deprived of their rights, of their very dignity as persons, they are *eo ipso* also released from their duties towards the social order, because this order is no longer their ethical substance: 'When a social order fails to actualize its own ethical principles, that amounts to the self-destruction of those principles.'[13] As is well known, this is the starting point of the Marxian analysis: the 'proletariat' designates such an 'irrational' element of the 'rational' social totality, an element systematically generated by it and, simultaneously, denied the basic rights that define this totality.

The problem with Strauss is the status of *his own* texts: are they also to be read in an esoteric way? Do they also contain a secret message to be deciphered? And how far do we go in this direction? What one should do here is not only resuscitate the boring self-referential paradoxes (how can Strauss directly disclose in public texts – published books – the secret which, according to his own teaching, should remain secret for the wider public?); it is insufficient to point out how his message is embarrassing and basically unacceptable to American neoconservatives who will never publicly state that there is no God and eternal justice, that they really do not believe in all these things. The key question is elsewhere: *what, precisely, is the 'esoteric' teaching of Strauss's books – say, of his* Persecution and the Art of Writing, *which is about the need to distinguish the exoteric and the esoteric message of great works?* There is only one consistent solution: the 'esoteric' teaching here can be only the insufficiency of the very distinction between exoteric and esoteric: namely, the scandalous fact that *there is more truth in the exoteric 'public' teaching than in the esoteric secret*, that the very writers who endeavour to dupe the uneducated by encoding their true message are, in their turn, the ones who are truly duped. What, then, if the true secret of the Straussians (and, perhaps, of Strauss himself) is not their secret disbelief, their cruel Nietzschean world-view, but their disavowed *belief*? The same goes even for Hitler – even a superficial reading of *Mein Kampf* leaves us perplexed when we try to answer a simple question: does Hitler believe himself or not? The only consistent answer is: both yes and no. On the one hand, it is clear that Hitler consciously 'manipulates': sometimes – for example, when he emphasizes how, in order to dominate the crowds and arouse their passions, one should present them with a simplified image of the one great Enemy on whom all the blame is put – he even directly shows his hand. On the other, it is no less clear that he gets passionately immersed in his own lore.

And perhaps the nostalgic longing permeating Strauss's writings is precisely the yearning for the (premodern) period when the simple opposition between esoteric and exoteric was still sustainable.[14] This is where the liberal paranoia about the neo-Straussian conspiracy of the ideological group controlling the Bush administration falls short. If anything, the Straussian neocons bring out the implicit paradox of Strauss's teaching: they *bring into public view* the difference between the public lie and the secret truth. That is to say: is there still, in the contemporary USA, an elite which clearly sees things the way they are? The first problem is that the distinction between the 'beautiful lie' for the general public and the bitter truth appropriate only for the elite is much too naive to describe what is going on today: this distinction itself is already part of public discourse. Recall the quote from Paul Wolfowitz cited in the Introduction, where he not only dismissed the WMD issue as a 'bureaucratic' excuse for war, but openly admitted that oil was the true motive: 'Let's look at it simply. The most important difference between North Korea and Iraq is that economically, we just had no choice in Iraq. The country swims on a sea of oil.'[15] Furthermore, there are clear signs of chaotic confusion among the elite. In July 2003, it was reported that the Pentagon was planning to spend tens of millions of dollars to set up a stock-market-style system in which investors would bet on terror attacks, assassinations and other events in the Middle East; in this way, defence officials hoped to gain intelligence and useful predictions, while investors who guessed correctly would reap profits. Investors would buy and sell futures contracts – essentially a series of predictions about what they believed might happen in the Middle East (the likelihood that Yasser Arafat might be assassinated, or that the Jordanian King Abdullah II might be overthrown). The holder of a futures contract that was fulfilled would collect the proceeds of investors who put money into the market but predicted wrongly. (Democratic Senator Byron Dorgan described this idea as useless, offensive and 'unbelievably stupid': 'Can you imagine if another country set up a betting parlor so that people could go in . . . and bet on the assassination of an American political figure, or the overthrow of this institution or that institution?') What did the

Pentagon expect to learn from this game? Would this game not, in a kind of closed loop, only reflect back the predominant opinion generated by the media?

The trap into which Strauss falls is thus the trap of all great 'demystifiers': his problem is not that he tries to return to classical political thought in the era of modernity, and can do so only by asserting the mechanism of the 'beautiful lie' sustained by brutal esoteric knowledge; his problem is, rather, that this very distinction between the exoteric 'beautiful lie' and the esoteric terrifying truth, daring and shocking as it may appear, is hopelessly dated and traditional. When Strauss reads Plato against the background of his 'secret teaching', we should not forget to apply to this the lesson of Lacan's *Kant avec Sade*. 'Kant with Sade' does not mean that Sade is the truth of Kant, that Sade is more consistent, and draws all the consequences of the Kantian revolution; on the contrary, the Sadeian perversion emerges as the result of the Kantian compromise, of Kant's avoidance of the consequences of his own breakthrough. In short, the core of the Kantian philosophical revolution is the insight into how *the absolute excess is that of the Law itself* – the Law intervenes in the 'homogeneous' stability of our pleasure-orientated life as the shattering force of absolute destabilizing 'heterogeneity'. The moral Law is thus no longer the agency which serves as a limitation, preventing us from going too far; it is the Law itself, its injunction, which is the ultimate 'transgression' of an idiotic life of modest pleasures – which is why, for Lacan, the moral Law is a name for desire as the excessive force which undermines the homeostatic reign of the pleasure principle. Measured by this Kantian standard, the Sadeian pervert is therefore a strictly *sublime* figure: his wildest transgressions belong to the empirical 'pathological' domain; they display the failed attempts of the pleasure-orientated empirical imagination to translate the noumenal (trans-phenomenal) Law into the domain of pleasure-orientated activity (just as, in the dynamic Sublime, the wildest display of the raging forces of nature reveals – in a negative way, through its very failure adequately to represent the noumenal moral Law – this dimension of the Law).

In other words, while Kant asserts the Law itself as the ultimate transgression (of our 'normal' life), Sade endeavours to translate this force of the Law back into the traditional opposition of the Law and its transgression – that is to say, his notion of the moral Law is still that of the agency of constraint and proper measure, which can be (and should be for Sade) undermined through an erotic-destructive excess. The sublime lesson of Sadeian perversion is thus not 'even the most excessive debauchery is impotent in the face of a firm moral stance' but, on the contrary, 'even the most excessive criminal debauchery cannot approach the infinite violent excess, the traumatic cut, of the moral Law itself'. Sade is 'the truth of Kant' only in the sense that he forces a Kantian to confront the unprecedented radicality of his own position: Sade is not so much the truth of Kant as the symptom of a compromise, the sign that Kant did not draw all the consequences from his philosophical revolution – for once a Kantian does follow through all these consequences, the figure of Sade loses its fascination, and becomes a ridiculous outdated spectacle.

When we read Sade, we cannot avoid the impression that we are reading a description of events with which we cannot psychologically identify: the described events are not only ridiculously exaggerated (like mutual simultaneous anal penetration with the penises of two men), but also brutally disgusting, preventing (for most of us, at least) any sexually arousing identification – Sade's text is either a boring mechanical exercise or a repellent catalogue of perversions. It is this very impossibility of identifying with the described events psychologically, however, that bears witness to the properly Kantian 'purity' of Sade: the Sadeian text is 'beyond the pleasure principle', it addresses itself to a 'non-pathological' subject in Kant's sense, a subject beyond the grasp of empirical-psychological dreams, passions, emotions and fears.

Sade is obsessed with the notion that natural laws themselves are the ultimate limit and challenge to human freedom, and that the supreme act is therefore to commit a crime so horrible that it would violate natural laws themselves. This is uncannily similar to Kant's central problem: is a human being free – free in the precise sense of the ability to commit an autonomous act, an act that is not conditioned by the natural chain of causes and effects? The most common definition of sadism – pleasure in inflicting pain – also echoes Kant's insight that, in the experience of the sublime, pleasure is mixed with pain: that is to say, what provides satisfaction is the very painful failure of our imagination to represent the noumenal. Also, as Lacan has noted, the only a priori (non-pathological) emotion is pain – the pain the subject experiences when his pathological self feels thwarted and crushed under the pressure of the moral law. In Sade's *Philosophy in the Boudoir*, Dolmance summons Eugénie 'to drown in floods of fuck the heavenly fire that blazes in us' – this was written during the period when Hölderlin was deploying the notion of poets as those who are afflicted by the 'fire from heaven'.

On a more general level, the notion of the positive, constitutive status of so-called forbidden knowledge – that is, the idea that, in order to attain the full satisfaction of our desire, its direct fulfilment should be postponed, even renounced – is more complex than it may appear. On a first approach, the very distance which separates us from the object, the fact that the object is visible and accessible only through the distorting lenses of prohibitions and obstacles, generates the magical aura which makes it so fascinating: were we to get a direct look at the object, we would soon perceive that it is just a common vulgar thing. It thus seems that we are dealing here with the common wisdom according to which it is the obstacle itself which sustains our desire: it is the prohibition as such which elevates a common everyday object into an object of desire – what makes it an object of desire is not its direct inherent properties, but the structural place it occupies. In other words, the very inaccessibility of the object, the fact that my perception of the object is imperfect, partial, full of blanks and voids, sets in motion my imagination, which fills in these blanks. Are there not already dozens of proverbs which make this point? The other man's grass is always greener, and so on. The status of forbidden knowledge, however, is more paradoxical: the key fact is that, in order to be operative, the prohibition has to be reflectively redoubled: the prohibition itself should be prohibited; in other words, it should not appear as such, in its positive dimension, but as a simple external obstacle which prevents us gaining access to the desired object. That is to say: I cannot tell myself, with regard to a woman with whom I am passionately in love: 'It's not really her, she's just a common ordinary girl – it's the aura of transgression, of entering a prohibited domain, which makes her so attractive; it's the force and excess of my imagination over her reality!' Such a direct insight is clearly a kind of 'pragmatic contradiction' which, when it is effectively assumed, ruins my desire. Truly forbidden knowledge is thus not the full knowledge of the reality of the beloved, but the very knowledge that there is *nothing* to learn about the reality of the object, that what makes the object the cause of my desire is the prohibited place it occupies.

In a homologous way, the same goes for the functioning of prohibitions under Stalinism: what was prohibited was not only the public (or any other, for that matter) critique of the ruling regime, but, even more, the public enunciation of this very prohibition. So when the accused in a Stalinist show trial confessed his rejection of Communist rule, it is not enough to say that we are dealing with a kind of 'return of the repressed', or that he publicly stated the prohibited secret desire of the majority; what was much more crucial was that those who publicly criticized Communist rule revealed the inconsistency of the ruling ideology: they practised not a prohibited right (to free speech) but one that was publicly guaranteed and secretly prohibited.

This is why the stance of maintaining a proper distance towards the beloved object in order not to disturb its spell is a sure sign of false love: true love is not 'afraid to get too close', it is a readiness to accept the beloved object in all its common reality and, *simultaneously*, retain its sublime status – or, to paraphrase Hegel's paraphrase of Martin Luther, *to recognize the rose of the sublime in the cross of everyday vulgarity.*

And the political lesson (or, rather, implication) of this stance of 'recognizing the rose of the sublime in the cross of everyday vulgarity' is not to mystify the existing reality, to paint it with false colours, but quite the contrary: to summon up the strength to translate the sublime (utopian) vision into everyday practice — in short, to *practise* utopia.

Notes

Introduction

1. Interestingly, Kay himself offered three theories for the failure to find the WMDs: (1) the WMDs are in Iraq; it is just that Saddam, the 'master of deceit', hid them well; (2) the WMDs are not in Iraq, because Saddam moved them outside the country just before the war; (3) Saddam never had them at all, and just bluffed to appear strong. (And, curiously, there is an additional eccentric twist: Saddam's scientists were fooling Saddam himself, and were simply too afraid to tell him he did not possess any weapons . . .). Incidentally, opponents of the war seemed to repeat the same inconsistent logic: (1) it is all really about the control of oil and American hegemony – the true rogue state which terrorizes others is the USA; (2) even if it is not only about oil and hegemony and the attack is justified, since Saddam is a murderer and torturer, and his regime a criminal catastrophe, it will be counter-productive – it will give a big boost to a new wave of anti-American terrorism; (3) even if it is successful, the attack on Iraq destined to overthrow Saddam will cost too much, and the money could be better spent elsewhere. . . .

2. As is well known, after her capture, Jessica was saved by al-Rehaief, an Iraqi doctor who took special care of her in the hospital. When, after the war, Dr al-Rehaief went to Palestine, West Virginia (*nomen omen!*) to visit Jessica, he was in for a series of nasty surprises. Jessica was too busy with preparations for the publicity campaign for her

book of memoirs on her captivity (in which he features as her saviour) to receive him. Then, to add insult to injury, the citizens of Palestine prepared a big reception feast for Dr al-Rehaief, unaware that it was Ramadan and that Dr al-Rehaief had to fast (not to mention the fact that they served fine local ham). So much for American gratitude and sensibility.

3. Of course, one can also say that both these approaches are the two sides of the perspective of the attacking invading force – the missing dimension is the perspective of the other side, the suffering and chaos among the bombarded Iraqis themselves, the perspective provided by al-Jazeera TV. What we got on Western TV instead were the surreal green night-time shots of Baghdad with the white-yellowish bomb explosions, like scenery from some abstract video game, so that the predominant opposition is the 'embedded' concrete experience of 'our guys fighting there' versus the abstract character of the destruction inflicted as pure pyrotechnics.

4. See George Wright, 'Wolfowitz: Iraq war was about oil', *The Guardian*, 4 June 2003.

5. Quoted from the *International Herald Tribune*, 22 October 2003, p. 8.

6. Ibid.

Non Penis a Pendendo

1. Indeed, the desperate search for WMDs is now reaching comical proportions, with the USA even offering financial rewards for any relevant information – so, after waging a war, there is now a competition with a prize for those who locate a reason for the war. ... Amusingly, one US diplomat even seriously suggested that one reason why the Iraqis had not used WMDs during the war was that they had concealed them so well that they themselves could not find and use them in time!

2. The recent debate on who should play the key role in ruling Iraq, the UN or the USA and their allies, shows the deep ethical-political

confusion of Europeans who want a key role for the UN. The military victory was the easy part, and now, instead of helping the USA and its allies to sort out the mess they have got themselves into, they should let them assume full responsibility for fulfilling their inflated promises.

3. This hypocrisy is matched only by the hypocrisy of the state of Israel blaming Arafat for not crushing the terrorism of Hamas – the same Hamas which, until recently, was financially supported by Israel with the Machiavellian goal of undermining the predominant influence of Arafat's PLO among the Palestinians – first you support Hamas, helping it to establish itself as a force out of Arafat's control, then you criticize Arafat for not controlling it. . . .

4. Quoted in *The Independent*, 30 October 2003, p. 15.

5. Concerning Hitchens, I have to confess a fundamental sympathy with him: although I disagree with his stance on Iraq, and on the war on terror, I infinitely prefer him to standard liberal-leftist anti-American 'pacifism'. Hitchens is an adversary worth reading – in contrast to many critics of the war on Iraq, who are much better ignored.

6. I pass over in silence Chirac's properly *racist* outbursts against the post-Communist Eastern European states which supported the USA in its war on Iraq.

7. G.K. Chesterton, *Orthodoxy*, San Francisco: Ignatius Press 1995, pp. 146–7.

8. I owe this information to Udi Aloni, New York.

9. So what if – to push this further – the very notion, found already in Ancient Greece (Tiresias), of how feminine sexual pleasure is seven times stronger than male (multiple orgasms, and so on) is sustained by women to make men envious?

10. Élisabeth Roudinesco, 'Homosexuality Today: A Challenge for Psychoanalysis?', *Journal of European Psychoanalysis* 15 (Fall–Winter 2002), p. 184.

11. Alain Badiou, *Infinite Thought*, London: Continuum 2003, p. 153.

12. And does not the same hold for the standard criticism of Lacanians: that they are 'dogmatic'? When deconstructionists criticize Lacanians for being too 'dogmatically' attached to Lacan, what they mean is that there is a 'dogmatic' kernel which defines the very core of

Lacanian theory – this is why 'dogmatically Lacanian' *simply means 'Lacanian'*. Is this not the only consistent explanation of the simple positive fact that the 'dogmatic' Lacanians are actually much more critical of Lacan in their texts than the standard deconstructionist is of Derrida? This, of course, does not mean that the reproach of 'Lacanian dogmatism' is without foundation: what it implicitly refers to is the crucial fact that Lacanian theory involves a radically different type of collectivity from deconstructionism: while deconstruction perfectly fits the existing academic machine, with its endless interpretative circulation, Lacanian theory involves the type of collective of engaged subjects found also in radical religious sects and/or revolutionary parties.

13. Ernst Nolte, *Martin Heidegger – Politik und Geschichte im Leben und Denken*, Berlin: Vittorio Klostermann Verlag 1992, p. 296.

14. Ibid , p 277

15. We encounter the same paradox in Adorno's treatment of the 'authoritarian personality': what is the status of a scale which contains features that are the opposite of those defining the 'authoritarian personality'? Are they simply to be endorsed as the 'democratic personality' (ultimately the path of Habermas), or is the 'authoritarian personality' to be conceived of as the symptomal 'truth' of the 'democratic personality' (the view of, say, Agamben)? This undecidability is ultimately a special case of the more general undecidability of the 'dialectic of Enlightenment' itself, well perceived by Habermas: if the 'administered world' is the 'truth' of the project of Enlightenment, how, precisely, can it be criticized and counteracted by way of fidelity to the Enlightenment project itself? I would be inclined to claim that, far from standing for an aporia or a simple failure on Adorno's part, this reluctance to take the step into the positive normativity indicates his fidelity to the Marxist revolutionary project.

16. For a succinct articulation of this position, see Judith Butler, 'No, It's Not Anti-Semitic', *London Review of Books*, 21 August 2003, pp. 19–21. No wonder, then, that Butler recently produced such a Rortyan statement: 'Perhaps, our chance to become human is precisely in the way we react to injuries' (quoted in the promotional page for Butler's *Kritik der ethischen Gewalt*, Suhrkamp catalogue for Summer 2003).

17. See Heinz Hoehne, *The Order of the Death's Head: The Story of Hitler's SS*, Harmondsworth: Penguin 2000, pp. 336–7.

18. The predicament of today's Germany clearly displays the limits and dangers of globalization: in the Federal Republic of Germany, the welfare state survived more or less intact, rendering its economy less competitive and flexible. The necessary 'restructuring' of the economy (the dismantling of the welfare state) encounters strong opposition from the majority of voters (workers, retired people . . .), so it can be enacted only by *non-democratic* means.

19. Gary Wills, 'Scandal', *The New York Review of Books*, 23 May 2002, p. 6.

20. G. K. Chesterton, 'A Defense of Detective Stories', in H. Haycraft, ed., *The Art of the Mystery Story*, New York: The Universal Library 1946, p. 6.

21. Fareed Zakaria, *The Future of Freedom*, New York: Norton 2003.

22. Kenneth Anderson, 'Who Owns the Rules of War?', *The New York Times Magazine*, 13 April 2003, pp. 38–43.

23. Henri Bergson, *Oeuvres*, Paris: PUF 1991, pp. 1110–11.

24. Ibid.

25. Ibid., p. 1340.

26. Jacques Lacan, *Les quatre concepts fondamentaux de la psychanalyse*, Paris: Éditions du Seuil 1973, p. 89.

Appendix I: Canis a non Canendo

1. See Karl Marx, 'Class Struggles in France', *Collected Works*, vol. 10, London: Lawrence & Wishart 1978, p. 95.

2. Susan Neiman, *Evil in Modern Thought*, Princeton, NJ: Princeton University Press 2002, p. 285.

3. Ibid., pp. 280–81.

4. Jürgen Habermas, *The Future of Human Nature*, Cambridge: Polity Press 2003, p. 110.

5. See the final pages of Ernest Larsen, *The Usual Suspects*, London: BFI 2002.

6. Yannis Stavrakakis, 'The Lure of Antigone', *Umbr(a)* 2003, p. 126.

7. For a clear articulation of this stance, see Martin Jay, 'No Power to the Soviets', in *Cultural Semantics*, Amherst: University of Massachusetts Press 1998.

8. William Taubman, *Khrushchev: The Man and His Era*, London: Free Press 2003, p. 493.

9. Chantal Mouffe, 'Religion, Liberal Democracy and Citizenship', in *ASCA Report 2001*, Amsterdam: Asca Press 2002, p. 110.

10. In his latest writings on populism, Laclau does perform this shift: populism versus democracy is now the ontological versus the ontic, in other words, democracy is the translation of populist antagonism into regulated agonism. In this way, however, the problem is merely transposed, since Laclau is well aware that populism can also cover proto-Fascist phenomena, so that reference to populism does not in any way provide an orientation that enables one to discern the 'progressive' character of a political movement.

11. Ernesto Laclau, 'Ethics, Normativity and the Heteronomy of the Law', unpublished manuscript.

12. Simon Critchley, 'Is There a Normative Deficit in the Theory of Hegemony?', quoted from http://www.essex.ac.uk./centres/TheoStud/papers/Laclau.

13. Ernesto Laclau, in *Hope*, ed. Mary Zournazi, London: Lawrence & Wishart 2002, p. 145.

14. Chantal Mouffe, in *Hope*, p. 129.

15. Ibid., p. 133.

16. See Joan Copjec, 'Euthanasia of Reason', in *Read My Desire*, Cambridge, MA: MIT Press 1995.

17. Alain Badiou, *L'être et l'évènement*, Paris: Éditions du Seuil 1988, p. 68.

18. Jacques Lacan, *La logique du fantasme* (seminar 1966–67), 10 May 1967.

19. See 'Lacan et la politique', interview with Jacques-Alain Miller, *Cites* 16/2003.

20. Transcription of the J.-P. Elkabbach telephone broadcast with J.-A. Miller and M. Accoyer, Europe 1, 10 October 2003, available on lacan.com.

21. Sigmund Freud, *Studienausgabe*, vol. III, Frankfurt: Fischer Verlag 2000, p. 384.

22. Yannis Stavrakakis, 'Re-Activating the Democratic Revolution', *Parallax*, vol. 9, no. 2, (2003), pp. 58, 62.

23. The catch here, of course, is the possibility of democratic fundamentalism – the Jacobins imposed their terror not as the natural embodiment of revolutionary power, but as the keepers of the empty place of power. (And, incidentally, after producing endless variations on the reversal of the lack of structure into a structure which in itself positivizes a lack, and so on, it is slightly annoying to be accused – by Laclau and Stavrakakis – of 'not seeing' how democracy is an institutionalization of lack, a political order which takes into account the ultimate contingency of political life!)

24. Jacques-Alain Miller, *Le Neveu de Lacan*, Paris: Verdier 2003, p. 270.

25. Ibid., pp. 146–7.

26. 'Lacan et la politique', p. 122.

27. Bertolt Brecht, *Gedichte in einem Band*, Frankfurt: Suhrkamp 1982, pp. 1009–10.

28. Bernard Williams, *Truth and Truthfulness*, Princeton, NJ: Princeton University Press 2002, pp. 7–8.

29. Bertolt Brecht, *Collected Plays: Three*, London: Methuen 1997, p. 87.

30. Ibid., p. 68.

31. *Truth and Truthfulness*, p. 125.

32. Ibid., p. 126.

33. Ibid., p. 130.

34. Quoted from Neil Harding, *Leninism*, Durham, NC: Duke University Press 1996, p. 309.

35. Ibid., p. 152.

Appendix II: Lucas a non Lucendo

1. I owe this point to Ken Rinehard, UCLA.

2. Lacan's formula of the signifier (a signifier represents the subject for all other signifiers) thus displays a structural homology with the Marxian formula of a commodity as also involving a dyad: the use-value of a commodity represents the value of another commodity. Even the variations in Lacan's formula can be systematized with reference to Marx's four forms of the expression of value (see Part 1 of Slavoj Žižek, *For They Know Not What They Do*, London: Verso 1991). Along these lines, it is crucial that Lacan determines the surplus-remainder of this process, *objet petit a*, as surplus-enjoyment [*plus-de-jouir*], in explicit reference to Marxian surplus-value.

3. See Jean Clavreuil, *L'ordre médical*, Paris: Éditions du Seuil 1975.

4. See Eric Santner, *My Own Private Germany*, Princeton, NJ: Princeton University Press 1996.

5. So, in the context of these considerations, in 1999, TV came to Shangri-la, Bhutan being the last country in the world finally to permit television – with the expected disastrous results (total decline of traditional culture, rise of violent crime).

6. In *Seminar XVII*, Lacan emphasizes the link between the rule of post-revolutionary *fraternité* and the logic of segregation.

7. I rely here on Giorgio Agamben, *L'état d'exception*, Paris: Éditions du Seuil 2003.

8. Élisabeth Roudinesco, 'Homosexuality Today: A Challenge for Psychoanalysis?', *Journal of European Psychoanalysis* 15 (fall–winter 2002), p. 184.

9. Leo Strauss, *Persecution and the Art of Writing*, Chicago: University of Chicago Press 1988 (first published 1952), p. 57.

10. Ibid., pp. 60–61.

11. Strauss, *Persecution and the Art of Writing*, pp. 178–9.

12. Ibid., pp. 62–3.

13. Allen W. Wood, *Hegel's Ethical Thought*, Cambridge: Cambridge University Press 1990, p. 255. Wood is fully justified in pointing out how the dismissive tone of Hegel's statements about the 'rabble' should not blind us to the basic fact that he considered their rebellion rationally fully justified: the 'rabble' is a class of people to whom recognition by the ethical substance is denied – systematically, not just in a contingent

way – so they do not owe anything to society either, and are excused any duties towards it.

14. Furthermore, is it not that, with regard to the classical period to which Strauss refers, today, the situation is, rather, reversed: the exoteric public view is that of the pursuit of pleasures, attachment to worldly goods, disbelief in any higher eternal moral order, etc., so that it is belief in divine justice, and so on, which has to be passed on as an esoteric secret which one does not dare to acknowledge in public?

15. See George Wright, 'Wolfowitz: Iraq war was about oil', *The Guardian*, 4 June 2003.